He Brought Me

OUT OF

the Miry

CLAY

and Set My Feet Upon a Rock

He Brought Me

OUT OF

the Miry

CLAY

and Set My Feet Upon a Rock

Jean Boustead

DESTINY IMAGE™ EUROPE srl
Via Maiella, 1
66020 San Giovanni Teatino (Ch) – Italy

"Changing the world, one book at a time."™

This book and all other Destiny Image™ Europe books are available at Christian bookstores and distributors worldwide.

To order products, or for any other correspondence:

DESTINY IMAGE™ EUROPE srl
Via della Scafa 29/14
65013 Città Sant'Angelo (Pe) – Italy
Tel. +39 085 4716623 • +39 085 8670146
Fax +39 085 9090113
Email: info@eurodestinyimage.com
Or reach us on the Internet: www.eurodestinyimage.com

ISBN 13: 978-88-96727-23-2
ISBN 13 Ebook: 978-88-96727-82-9
For Worldwide Distribution, Printed in Italy
1 2 3 4 5 6 / 14 13 12 11

Acknowledgments

Until the present I have only spoken about my past as God has given me liberty. I've now decided it is time for it to be made known as it is. Much of what I have written has never been told before. I have been honest and sincere when writing about the many people who are part of my story. It is my prayer that those who read it recognize this and that some may find God's goodness to me an encouragement.

I'd like to thank the stranger on the train who gave me a sheet of paper from his briefcase that enabled me to get started. My special gratitude goes to John, my husband and champion, who has cheered me all the way with endless faith, help, and love. To Paula, who pointed me to Lanark Writers, without whose support I could not have made it, especially Rebecca for her patience and guidance in the early days. Gratitude to my friends Pat, who not only proofread but coached and encouraged me, and Mavis, for proofreading and giving sound advice.

I wish to express my great appreciation to Andrew, the manager of GLO, our Christian bookshop in Motherwell, who not only proofread but gently pushed me to continue to write from the beginning, giving me encouragement and wise counsel. Thanks to those who have believed in me, telling me to write and the many unnamed friends who have offered the right word when I needed it. Also, special thanks to Grant who, at the last moment, expertly put the manuscript into a beautiful format that I could not have done myself, making it suitable for the publisher.

The encouragement and financial support from members of management in Mental Health Lanarkshire, Kevin, Anne-Marie, and Marian, has been deeply appreciated, as has been their friendship and commitment to enable my story to be used to help others.

Penultimate thanks to my son, Matthew, who resuscitated my old, dying computer just in time and saved me from fragmenting! His expertise was invaluable in helping me choose a new machine, making it possible to finish this work. He has made my story and life complete.

Finally, thank you Jesus, the Author and Finisher of our faith, for renewing my mind, restoring my soul and enabling me to recall events and accomplish what was to me an insurmountable mountain.

Endorsements

Jean Boustead has written the story of her life, and she has made a very good job of it. She has had a good deal of illness, and has spent time in hospital. She has also discovered the truth of her Christian faith and has set it forth with force and skill. She writes with frankness and charity and in such a way that we may all benefit from reading her narrative. I very much hope that this honest and searching book will be read by very many of the public; they will certainly benefit from doing so.

Sir Robin Barbour
Former Moderator of the Church of Scotland
Former Chaplain to the Queen

Jean Boustead's powerful, well-written life story touched me deeply. This book joins the ranks of thousands of testimonies of broken, desperate, hopeless women who met Jesus and were changed forever. He indeed knows and sees our hidden sorrow and gives lasting joy!

Anneke Companjen
Speaker, Author
Open Doors International

We know that "there is nothing more powerful than the real life example that recovery from mental health problems can and does happen." Key to recovery is finding meaning and purpose in life, having a belief that recovery is possible, as well as having people around us who support and understand. For many people "meaning and purpose" is found in life in other areas such as volunteering, family and community whether the person has a faith or not. However, we know that spirituality plays a very important part in both community and individual mental health and well-being. Jean's story describes her life and recovery as a journey with ups and downs. Her personal testimony frames her recovery within the context of her faith which many people who are experiencing mental health problems will be able to relate to, and draw hope from. Jean has given the gift of herself in sharing her life story and indeed reminds us that recording our stories helps us to make sense of our life and sharing it helps others benefit from our experiences. Thank you Jean.

Kevin O'Neill,
Public Mental Health & Well-being Development Manager

Contents

Foreword

We heal in relationships, and the Christian would add that the Author of all caring relationships is God, whereas the author of disrupted, dysfunctional relationships is satan.

Nowhere is this more apparent than this journey through Jean Boustead's life, where affirming relationships fostered growth, wholeness, and healing—while each time she engaged in dysfunctional relationships, it diminished her.

She undoubtedly faced enormous challenges from an early age, the legacy of her family looming large at every turn, resulting in her years of low self-esteem and damaging her capacity to engage in her own rewarding adult relationships.

So where did Jean's unreasonable hope come from that the secular world could never recognize. It came straight from God who had Jean's name written on His hand! He broke into her life disrupting everything that went before, and she experienced this unconditional love, "agape" love, a balm that healed her raw, open wounds. It was a love that gave and took nothing back, that sacrificed, that was patient as Jean struggled with herself and those around her.

The secular world deals with its bad experiences of the past by trying to forget them, but somewhere deep in the subconscious its rhythm still plays on like a tune you cannot get out of your head, imprisoning each new relationship with its destructive forces.

Meanwhile, Jean Boustead was a new creature. She could embrace her past and, with the support of her relationship with Jesus, fracture its harsh chains. That profound, loving relationship she experienced permitted the breakthrough of forgiving. Her identity was no longer defined by the vacuums in her life, by what she was not. It was now defined by what she was. It liberated her potential to become vulnerable, not defensive, inspired to be able to give love.

A wonderful parable of Jean's life struggle in nature is that life-or-death combat of the butterfly to free itself from the pupae—fly, Jean, fly!

Dave Clark
Head of Learning Disabilities Services
Church of Scotland

Introduction

It has been said that everyone has a story. A Christian, on looking back, sees that it is Another's story. This is how I feel. Often during my life I felt mine was different in many ways. Circumstances I was taken through were allowed, but were not my choice.

When I have been asked to give my testimony publicly or privately, I have been told to write. But where to start? Then one day while travelling home by train after visiting my small grandson, the Lord began to form a possible beginning in my mind. On seeing a man at the far end of the compartment with an open brief-case, I approached and asked him if he could spare a sheet of paper. He seemed delighted to oblige.

So it was that the first birth pangs of this book began. It has taken many years and I am grateful to the Lord that I have been able to recall events that were difficult and painful and know the guilt and pain have been healed. In fact, writing this has been a therapy.

I joined Lanark Writers, a writing group, to help me set it forth in a more acceptable form. At the same time I took a computer course and eventually qualified with an ECDL certificate. When I decided I had finished—if one ever does—I began contacting publishers; a daunting task. Then a book I was reading impressed me and caused me to look up the publisher, Destiny Image Europe. It took little effort to contact them and I soon found I was embarking on a wonderful, exciting journey.

When I realized the amount of money required to publish a book, I said quite honestly, "I don't have that kind of money." I was simply told, "That is not your problem." I believed God was speaking to me. After all, I only have the story. A happy exchange of communication took place for a year, with me still wondering how they could believe I could make it.

The manuscript was in disjointed chapters and I was asked to "stitch them together." I asked an experienced, but busy, friend who was about to have a holiday, how to do this. He took it on himself and set the manuscript out into a beautiful, continuous format.

When the contracts were sent to me I sought the advice of Christian lawyer friends. With suggested amendments made, I felt there was nothing I could find to stop me signing them. Eventually, I decided to step out and trust the Lord and Destiny Image Europe, and wait. The first thing was an unexpected tax rebate came in; with this we "got the show on the road." When the next amount for the process was needed I received a letter from a lawyer informing me a friend, who had just died, had left me a small inheritance. Robert had been in hospital with me and I had continued to visit him and occasionally befriend this dear man. It so blessed me that it had meant so much to him.

At one point, after I asked to speak to someone in Mental Health about another matter, I was introduced to the development manager in Mental Health Lanarkshire. During our conversation he expressed interest when I mentioned the book and, on reading the manuscript, was extremely encouraging and became involved, along with his colleagues, in assisting funding the final stages of the publication. The Lord has led and provided all the way.

Chapter One

Prisoner

> *Long my imprisoned spirit lay,*
> *Fast bound in sin and nature's night;*
> *Thine eye diffused a quickening ray;*
> *I awoke; the dungeon flamed with light.*
> *My chains fell off, my heart was free,*
> *I rose, went forth, and followed Thee.*
> —Charles Wesley[1]

The gate slammed and was locked behind us as we stepped through. Coiled barbed wire ran around the top of the high fence. We were led across the courtyard by guards and had to wait while our particulars were checked.

Prison was a revelation! I hadn't known what to expect.

Low Moss was a young offender's prison where we had been invited to take our visitor, a young man named Bright. He was to speak at the Prison Fellowship, a Christian program for inmates.

Bright, an African I met on a train, was attending Bible college. He was slight in stature, personable, intelligent, and a good speaker. He was almost like a member of our family, treating our home as his own and staying with us while on vacation from college.

"Can I bake some cakes for the men?" I asked the man who invited us.

"This is a prison. If they get fed cake, they'll only come to the Fellowship for the baking."

Slightly rebuked, I accepted this but then he said, "Oh well, I don't suppose it would hurt."

With a tin of rock cakes in my hand, we were led to a small building, the prison chapel. Waiting in the chapel I felt slight apprehension, not knowing what these men would look like or how we'd be received.

The door opened and about twenty fine-looking, young men filed in. They were all clean-shaven and dressed alike in burgundy sweat-shirts, with short, neatly cut hair. One by one they took their seats, sitting in a circle. Guards were present but not overly obvious.

The man who led the meeting introduced Bright.

We enjoyed a time of worship and sang several hymns and choruses lustily, with which they all seemed familiar. Bright spoke in an informal manner and they listened with interest and respect. As the meeting ended, they plied him with intelligent, searching questions about himself and what he had spoken on.

In the corner of the chapel, tea was brought in and poured into disposable cups. My tin of cakes was handed round, greeted by smiles. Afterward, over a cup of tea I talked with many of these young men. Perhaps the homey touch of the baking warmed them to me. They were certainly appreciative. They told me story after story of their circumstances and my heart went out to them. But I became aware that although they were physically restrained, they were mentally very agile and astute. An experienced friend explained that their minds became sharpened to achieve their own devious ends.

All of these men longed to be free. They believed they would change when they were released, vowing never to return. Many already had. What their chances were like on the outside is difficult to imagine. Several told me how they had lost the home life they previously enjoyed because their wives or partners were unable to cope with or believe in them anymore. They had regrets and fears. They were also very aware of reality, and there was a refreshing absence of pretence.

BEFORE CHRIST SET ME FREE, I HAD BEEN A PRISONER TO SIN, MYSELF, AND MY MIND—LOCKED TO THE WORLD AROUND ME.

I listened to them and as we talked, I found myself explaining to them that many people walking the streets, apparently free, are in fact in as much of a prison as they, but on the inside. I confessed to them that I had been in that type of prison before Christ set me free. I had been a prisoner to sin, myself, and my mind—locked to the world around me. They seemed to understand.

FREEDOM

What is freedom?

Freedom means to be free from something that binds, not necessarily to do something. To be able to choose what is right and not be a victim of one's own will and passion.

In Romans we read, "For the good that I will to do, I do not do; but the evil I will not to do, that I practice."[2] Many of us have known that condition.

I had felt, as these young prisoners did, that the answer must lie somewhere. I so wanted to be free and different. I didn't really know who I was.

In his daily reading book *Every Day with Jesus*, Selwyn Hughes says, "The only way to know ourselves is to know God and the only way to know God is when we know ourselves." I believe this to be absolutely true.

To be the person God wants you to be is to be free to love unselfishly.

Oswald Chambers, well-known author of *My Utmost for His Highest*, talks about being free in essence, free from the inside and how natural individuality is to be broken and our personality united with God.

These young men, like me, wanted to be set free.

GENERATIONS

I had suffered from mental illness, as my own mother and family members did before me. My upbringing had tended to be narrow and not particularly conducive in making me into an all-embracing, outgoing person. This was through no fault of my parents. Though to some outwardly I was a happy, respectable, confident young woman, on the inside I was in a straight jacket.

"...Who will deliver me from this body of death?" we read in Romans.[3]

Some people believe we are a product of our environment, others of heredity. I believe both. Certainly what happens in early life shapes or warps our personalities. But we not only inherit our physical appearances but often character traits and thought processes from our predecessors.

Abram said to Sarah, "Please say you are my sister...."[4] He was afraid he would be killed by the Egyptians if they knew she was his wife.

A generation later, Isaac, Abram's son, said about Rebekah, his wife, "She is my sister." He was afraid the men of the place might kill him because she was beautiful; thus betraying a family characteristic of not telling the truth.

Our DNA, they have discovered, denotes aspects of our makeup from conception and will often include involuntary makeup from our parents. Hence, we need God's DNA, which we can only get through new birth.

In John's Gospel it says, "Therefore if the Son makes you free, you shall be free indeed."[5] I felt sad as we left Low Moss knowing that the only answer to the plight of these young men was indeed Christ.

ENDNOTES

1. Charles Wesley, hymn, And Can It Be, 1738.

2. Romans 7:19.

3. Romans 7:24.

4. Genesis 12:13.

5. John 8:36.

Chapter Two

My Inner Journey

...Even though our outward man is perishing,
yet the inward man is being renewed day by day.[1]

Through the changing scenes of my journey my inner life has been deepened, often as a result of the many people whom God has brought across its path. It took the Lord several years to heal memories and restore my life to some normality. Wholeness didn't just happen at once.

I had most likely inherited my mental attitude from my mother. After her first breakdown,her fragile mental and nervous condition continued throughout the rest of her life. After my breakdown and following psychotic problems, it could have been a matter of course for me to have suffered in the same way. Many conditions are handed down, but I came to see that some are adopted. It is usually not possible to go further than a parent, a teacher, or even a pastor. We can't take anyone beyond where we are ourselves.

Mum was a worrier. She would expect the negative. She feared the unknown and had low self-esteem and little confidence. It is little wonder that I took on this temperament in my own makeup. After her first breakdown, she continued the rest of her life in that condition.

When I came to the point of accepting my own sin and state in repentance, I hated my life. So deep was the desire to be rid of all I had done and been, it was as if I performed an execution. When seeking His forgiveness God met me, the realization of His love, acceptance, and forgiveness sunk deep within me. It has never left me.

FORGIVENESS

Forgiveness is the bedrock of the Gospel. When we truly know we are forgiven, nothing else really matters. Unlike some, I never had to forgive myself; the fact that Jesus had forgiven me was enough. Later I was to learn the importance of forgiving others. On one occasion, when speaking to a ministering brother about a struggle I had, he said, "You do realize forgiveness is for your sake."

We leave the one we forgive, especially if they see no need to apologize, to God. He will deal with them. Through reading *Total Forgiveness*[2] by R.T. Kendall, God brought me into a deeper level where forgiveness was concerned. As I read this book I thought I had arrived!

Then something he wrote was new to me, and I thought, I am not there! I got before the Lord about it and it was as if He held a door open before me. He was on the other side of the door and was beckoning me through. The ground I was on was not sin, but I had to leave it and walk through. The choice was mine. I walked through the door and it was like my conversion experience in some ways; a fresh encounter with God!

We shouldn't get into bondage to forge a friendship with the person we have forgiven. Just let it all go. Although it is a continual process.

Patterns of a lifetime take a lot of changing; wrong reactions that arise have to be disciplined. I was so fortunate that God, in His merciful plan, placed me in the home and company of Norah, who I will speak about later. Not only was she a wonderful example as a spiritual woman, she was full of positive faith. Nothing seemed to throw her. I decided as far as possible to follow her example and adopt her attitude as closely as I could. It meant giving up my old way of thinking and, as situations arose, with my will, allowing God to alter my own reactions.

Norah once said to me, "Whatever is depressive or negative or pulls you down is from the devil—reject it! Whatever is of love, faith, and encouragement is from God—receive it!"

"WHATEVER IS DEPRESSIVE OR NEGATIVE OR PULLS YOU DOWN
IS FROM THE DEVIL—REJECT IT! WHATEVER IS OF LOVE, FAITH,
AND ENCOURAGEMENT IS FROM GOD—RECEIVE IT!"

We have to do the rejecting or accepting. All our lives we have the choice and the more we reject the negative and embrace the positive the stronger in spirit we become. This is how our minds are renewed. That has been my experience. Also, it is important what comes out of our mouths, for our own and for other's sake. I discovered it edifies to confess the positive and not the negative.

WORRY AND FEAR

Worry and fear go hand in hand.

Words by Mr. North, who will I mention later, also were life to me. He said, "Some fears are healthy. Fear stops us throwing a baby into a fire! It keeps us from stepping in front of a car!" The Bible says, "Perfect love casts out fear. (The wrong type of) fear has torment." Mr. North said, "Fear causes a person to act out of character!" and "The root of all fear is the fear of death." Thinking that through, it is absolutely right. We have to learn where fear comes from. Fear is the opposite of faith. Fear and worry are connected to our self life. We worry because we fear what will happen to us or what we are responsible for.

I came to see how limited my own perspective of things is. I worried because I couldn't see the answer. It didn't mean there wasn't an answer.

Jesus continually said, "Fear not." He wouldn't say that meaninglessly. He knew it was possible not to fear. If in His death Jesus took all of me to the cross, then what happens to me now is His responsibility. If I continually die to my right to myself and yield to His control, will He not take care of me and my concerns?

IF YOU CONTINUALLY DIE TO YOUR RIGHT TO YOURSELF
AND YIELD TO GOD'S CONTROL, WILL HE NOT TAKE CARE
OF YOU AND YOUR CONCERNS?

Our problem often is that we are seated on the throne of our life. When Jesus is given pre-eminence, He knows exactly what is best—for us and Him. I find that learning to give up my right to myself, to die and let Him have His way, takes time, practice, and will. He said, "If you lose your life, you will find it" (see Matt. 10:39). We lose it in Him and discover it anew in Him. Worry and fear will stop me, but while I continually die to myself I live in Him. I have found my relationship with Christ deepened with each difficult situation that otherwise would have worried me. Refusing the doubts, fears, and faces of man, I am learning to seek the face of Jesus over everything. Only on the basis of His unconditional love and in His presence can I let go of my inadequacies and receive His peace, by faith.

BE REAL WITH GOD

Mr. North also used to say, "Do business with God!" We have to transact with Him.

As time has gone on, I've realized what God thinks of me is of far more importance than what man thinks. I also found the love I knew in Christ satisfied me far more than any human love. Human love and relationships were an ability to express His love here on earth. That didn't mean it was always received. In fact, some relationships went wrong, and I couldn't understand why. Perhaps I appeared too intense—another lesson to learn.

If I seek to please my heavenly Bridegroom in every way as a woman, I'll not envy or try to emulate any earthly woman. I have seen several women as role models and sought to follow their example but even these are not complete in what Christ wants for me. To know I can dress how He wants me to look, keep my home to please Him, and spend my time doing what He wants, seeking His glory not my own, is for me the most satisfying, secure, and rewarding way to live.

Many lessons I have learned have been from godly men and women. Madame Guyon's books have taught me a lot about a deeper death to self. I can allow something unpleasant to crucify self and give place to Jesus instead of complaining. In Colossians 3:3 it says, "For you died, and your life is hidden with Christ in God."

I value what is going on inside me more than what is happening outside, most of the time. In a daily reading by Selwyn Hughes, he quoted a verse by someone,

> *Nothing that happens can harm me.*
> *Whether I lose or win.*

Though life may be changed on the surface
I do my main living within.[3]

He also once wrote, "Think with your mind, not your emotions!" This has proved valuable to me. Women, in particular, move from their emotions. Our emotions can't be relied upon.

In a message I listened to recently, Mr. North explained that we are building a house in our lives. What I build on the inside will be for eternity. Everything else will decay with this body on earth.

My prayer is that God will give me the strength to continue. He says He will carry us even into old age. If old age is a privilege I'm allowed, I look to Him for the grace to keep my mind stayed on Him. He gives me peace of mind. To rest in Him sometimes takes strength. Jesus was a meek person—not a weak one.

He says, "As your days, so shall your strength be" (Deuteronomy 33:25).

For our light affliction, which is but for a moment, is working for us a far more exceeding and eternal weight of glory (2 Corinthians 4:17).

ENDNOTES

1. 2 Corinthians 4:16.

2. R.T. Kendall, *Total Forgiveness* (Lake Mary, FL: Creation House).

3. Selwyn Hughes, *Author of Every Day with Jesus* daily reading books. Publication by CWR, Farnham, Surrey. UK.

Chapter Three

The Reunion

I know whom I have believed,
And am persuaded that He is able
To keep that which I've committed
Unto Him against that day.
—El Nathan, 1883

There was a sense of timelessness as we sat together drinking coffee. I had never believed this could be possible.

"Did you ever think of trying to find me?"...

~

The car turned into the little cobbled street in Leeds (borough of West Yorkshire in north-central England) and pulled up outside the small terrace house. Stepping out of the car I mounted the small flight of steps that took me to the front door. Anticipation mixed with uncertainty—yet hope filled me. It was autumn 1993. I was aware that I was standing on the threshold of a new era in my life.

The door was opened by Matthew. It was twenty-four years since I had seen my son, but I recognized him immediately. His smile assured and welcomed me. As I stepped forward, we hugged; then he led me into the small, modestly furnished living room. He was barely three when I had seen him for the last time. People have asked if it was an emotional reunion. Well, it wasn't really. For me, there was almost a feeling of coming home; completion. Yet I could hardly believe it was happening.

FOR ME, THERE WAS ALMOST A FEELING
OF COMING HOME, COMPLETION.

In meeting Matthew I wanted to see the man he had become, and what the outcome had been of my letting him go so long ago. I wanted to confirm that I had done the right thing by seeing the end result. To a great extent, I was satisfied.

I had been driven by Mickey, the pastor of the little Christian Fellowship I attended in Scotland, where I lived. An outgoing Scot, Mickey Wright had been a great source of support through many situations. As I introduced them, Matthew said to Mickey, "Thank you for doing the honors." Mickey stayed for a short time and, noticing Matthew's guitar in the corner, chatted about music in which they discovered they both shared an interest. This helped bring an ease to the atmosphere and conversation.

Mickey took Matthew's phone number, and it was agreed he would phone in a couple of hours. He returned to his wife, who was waiting in the home of a couple we knew. Chris was also a pastor of a Fellowship in Leeds where we had all eaten lunch before he led the way to Matthew's address.

Over all the years since I last saw Matthew, I had thought about my son, wondering, if not worrying. It wasn't his physical appearance that was of concern but what his personality would be like. Would he have grown up with a chip on his shoulder? Would he be hard, or worse still, bitter? Most important still to me, would he have been spared the inherited mental problems that were evident in my own family?

RECONNECTING

Matthew was brought up in Norfolk by his father, who had remarried; he told me he hadn't lived in this present house long. It took the Salvation Army just six weeks to find my son. Certainly Leeds was a lot nearer to Scotland than Norfolk. The letter from the Salvation Army had been delivered to a different address at first, where he had previously lived, he told me. He discovered it on a visit. I found this encouraging.

We soon began to ask each other questions. There seemed so much to ask but where do you begin? I wanted to study him and my eyes followed him whenever he left the room. His dark hair was long, in a pony tail. He was slight and dressed like any young man of his age. This gentle-natured young man who sat across the room from me filled me with a pride I felt I didn't deserve. I felt grateful for the way his father and stepmother had brought him up.

I asked about his paternal grandparents and learned that my former mother-in-law was dead. He then updated me on other family members.

"What was your stepmother like?" I enquired.

"Firm," he said.

He had a half-sister with whom he was obviously close. His relationship with his father was good, and he had taken up plumbing after him.

"Did you have any childhood illnesses?" I asked.

"I broke my leg falling from a swing."

I found myself wishing I could have been there for him.

"Did you find it difficult knowing your stepmother wasn't your real mother?"

He said he hadn't known she wasn't his real mother until he was about ten years old.

"No, but I did have three sets of grandparents."

I wondered what he had been told about me, "Did you ever think of looking for me?"

"Not really, but I tried to recognize you from photos I've seen of you as you arrived."

Many years later he told me whenever he considered looking for me he would wonder what I'd be like and whether I would be stricter than his stepmother.

We drank several cups of strong coffee as we talked. I took out his baby photographs that I had brought with me. We looked at them together, and I asked him to choose one. He chose my favorite. In it he was wearing a pale blue siren suit with a pointed hood with a pom-pom, and smiling happily. He had been a happy baby and the photos were full of smiles.

At one point Matthew disappeared upstairs. I couldn't have dreamed what was about to happen next. He returned to the room where I sat, holding out a handsome teddy bear.

"Do you remember him?" he asked.

I stared in amazement and delight, my mind recalling with pain, "Of course I do. I bought him for your first Christmas."

The teddy bear was still in beautiful condition and had obviously been treasured. It somehow linked the past and the present together. I felt thrilled that he had kept it all those years, yet hurt because of all the years I had missed. My imagination strained to envision him with it as he grew up.

When eventually Mickey phoned, I was encouraged that Matthew said, "Give us another half-hour."

On his return to collect me and as we left, Mickey offered, "If you'd like a holiday in Scotland and your mum can't put you up, you can always stay with us."

"I might take you up on that; I've never been to Scotland," Matthew said.

While Mickey had been away and we were alone, Matthew and I had talked, comparing events leading up to the meeting, discovering things about each other and what had taken place during the years that passed while we had been apart.

"Did anyone tell you what happened?" I asked, referring to my giving him up.

"Nobody has ever told me anything."

"Would you like me to tell you?"

"It would help…"

Chapter Four

Memories of London

When I was a child, I spoke as a child,
I understood as a child,
I thought as a child.[1]

"I've not always been old," my friend, Jo used to say. She was in her eighties.

"Be careful, you nearly hit that old lady!" the little boy said, as the ball came over the fence, while I walked past a school. I was just fifty then!

≈

LIFE AS A CHILD

The streets in London were quiet and, as children, we could play in them without fear. Brixton, where we lived, was different from what it is now. Front doors could be left on a latch or just unlocked.

My childhood days seem almost forgotten and many of the ensuing years another world away. Brought up in London, I realize that life then although not very affluent, was simpler and safer. We lived in the upper two floors of a large Victorian-style terrace, with a friendly family on the lower floors. My father worked hard as a postman to provide for us, saving to buy the house he hoped for one day. I had one brother, Bill, who was almost four years older than me. Apart from having two children,

Dad kept caged birds in a corner of the front room and a large aquarium of tropical fish. At times, some of these became game for my cat.

The house we lived in didn't have a bathroom. In the corner of the kitchen-living room sat a crock sink that had only a cold water tap. A metal bathtub was kept on the upstairs landing. Every Friday was bath night for the whole family when the tub was moved into the kitchen. It was then filled with hot water from the boiler in which Mum did her washing. One by one we would bathe in the kitchen; and in the winter, the sides of the tub would get hot beside the open fire. There were coal fires then and these caused "pea-soupers"—dense smog that hung in the air and choked and blinded us.

It was the Queen's Coronation in 1953 that prompted many people to buy a television. Until then we didn't have one. Television then only had programs for a few hours in the evenings, which were all very innocent. Before that, families would listen to "the wireless," as the radio was known. Saturday mornings were spent going to the children's matinee at the cinema. It cost 6 old pence (about 2 new pence) to get in, and we would cheer our heroes and boo the baddies.

One game we played as children was called Tin can Tommy; like hide-and-seek with a tin can at base. Hopscotch and Rounders were played on the road. Hardly anyone had a car back then. Although as a little girl I became a Brownie, later I outgrew the Girl Guides. I left, giving too much homework as an excuse. A few weeks later, sitting on a park bench with a boyfriend, the entire Guide pack walked past, "No homework, tonight?" called the guide captain!

THE CALL OF GOD

I attended a Sunday school. This was run by the Christadelphians. In those days it was the "thing to do," irrespective of family beliefs. Possibly parents saw this as a way of having a break from their children as there weren't the forms of entertainment that came later.

I felt the people who taught us had something, and it stirred something within me when I heard them talk about Jesus. A desire for God crept into my heart.

I remember so well the first time I heard the story of the child Samuel and how he heard God's voice calling him by name in the night. Only Eli the priest realized it was God, after Samuel questioned Eli for the third time, and he told Samuel to say, "Speak Lord, Thy servant heareth."[2] Going home afterward I went to my bedroom and was so disappointed that, when lying on my bed and repeating these words myself, I didn't hear God speak to me, as Samuel had.

The fact that God had heard me wasn't something I realized then. In those days, there was a feeling that God was so far away and I had a sort of fear of Him, perhaps instilled by my father who often spoke of his unhappy days in a convent school and the bad experiences which affected his attitude.

The desire for God remained dormant in my heart.

OUR FAMILY

My brother Bill and I were evacuated with our mother during World War II to live in St. Helens in Lancashire, boarding a train with a luggage label pinned to our coats. It was not an easy time for Mum. We were given a room in a large house along with the family whose house it was. The ivy-covered wall of the drive to this house is something I can still picture, along with the frogs that escaped when Bill hid his tadpoles under the ivy when he wasn't allowed to bring them into the house.

Soon after we returned to London, Dad came back from the war. He hadn't seen us since we were toddlers and I was then about four. I can remember seeing him in his uniform with his kit bag. As children we would play on bomb sites; actually in the shells of bombed houses. There were no green fields around us, just piles of bricks and rubble. The weed-covered remnants of gardens still bore the odd shrub. These sites weren't fenced off; there were too many. We were able to play quite freely, and one's imagination could run riot exploring these ruins, with the evidence of lives lived in them.

IMAGINATIONS COULD RUN RIOT EXPLORING THESE RUINS,
WITH THE EVIDENCE OF LIVES LIVED IN THEM.

Being born during the war and very young in the post war years, I still have memories of rationing. Many things were scarce; food such as meat, eggs and especially sugar, and clothing. Women learned to sew and make do. This did me no harm as I learned skills from my mother how to live on very little. She taught me how to cook, sew, and knit, and I continued to enjoy these skills as a means of relaxation as well as economy in future years.

Our parents did their best for us. Their own lives had been hard. Love was not something I was ever aware of being mentioned or demonstrated in the home; neither was any form of religious practice. In fact, Dad was quite bitter where God was concerned and professed to being an atheist. I don't think Mum really knew what she believed. She was a simple, home-loving person who could turn her hand to most things of a domestic nature and was very thrifty. Small in stature, she was matronly in shape with auburn hair. Dad was heavier and had been quite handsome. He still had a nice face with receding dark hair.

Mum was an emotional person. When my brother got married very young, she didn't seem able to handle it. She had her first breakdown when I was about sixteen. That was the first time I had to visit her in a mental hospital. She had periods when she coped and seemed well but was quite fragile. She was hospitalized on a number of occasions. The one I found hardest was when I was about nineteen; I was sent for from work three days before Christmas, as she had taken an overdose.

I was aware of a form of loneliness as a child, and I didn't find solitude comfortable. I've discovered others have experienced this, wondering what life was all about. As my friend remarked later, these were feelings like homesickness. At times it made me cry. As children Bill and I were not very close. Our lives and personalities were different from each other. He married young, and as adults we drifted apart.

We were not an academic family. Dad was a keen gardener and nature lover. My brother inherited these interests; whereas I was perhaps a bit more creative by nature and enjoyed things like art. Reading in those days wasn't something I found I could concentrate on.

Overstating my age, I applied for a paper-round in my early teens. It was a long walk to the paper shop, which meant I had to get up soon after 5:30 a.m. In the winter, it was very dark, walking alone. Returning home later I would wash and change, and on Saturdays and school holidays I went on to work in C & A, the well known high-street clothes shop. I wanted to buy everything in the store. The staff had a rail to put things on that they wanted to buy. I did this continually; but by the end of the week I had enjoyed admiring them, so was content to just put them back. Well, most of them.

My teenage years were fairly normal. Normal, except that I felt I always had to have a boyfriend, someone to belong to. It would be quite usual in those days to go to some kind of dance at the weekends, which I loved. Social dances were held in church halls. These would have a band playing modern music. Only soft drinks then would have been served, and admission was free. More sophisticated dances would be held in formal halls. Afterward we would either walk home or catch a bus. No young person owned a car then or had parents who did.

I ALWAYS HAD TO HAVE A BOYFRIEND, SOMEONE TO BELONG TO.

I had aunts and uncles, but we were not close in relationships or distance. We didn't see them very often, except for one of Mum's sisters, Aunt Glad, her husband Jack, and two cousins, Mike and Barry. Our maternal grandmother wasn't alive and Granddad lived in Folkestone, Kent, which was about 50 miles from London. My grandparents on my father's side lived in Shepherd's Bush, London and we only saw them occasionally. Granddad was a Glaswegian and never lost his strong Scottish accent. My maiden name was actually Jean Macnab. I was named after Dad's Aunt Jean. On one occasion, when I was about seven years old, we all went to visit our relatives in Scotland. It was quite a clan gathering, many dressed in our own tartan.

As a family we would often go out into the country on weekends by bus. Possibly living in London, the transport was more frequent and, Mum explained later, that living in a flat in the city gave them a desire to get us out and about whenever possible.

I was in my last year at school when Dad bought a house in Peckham. He had always talked of owning a house one day for us as a family, but Bill had already left home and was married by the time we moved into it.

PREPARATION FOR LIFE

I wasn't brilliant at school. There were subjects I enjoyed more than others. We had a very good English teacher whom I remember with gratitude. She helped me appreciate our language and encouraged us to express ourselves by using it. She was our form mistress too, and as a person she inspired me. Her quiet demeanour and modest, self effacing manner was an example to us all. The fact that she married the maths master didn't give me a love of maths. It remained my worst subject. He found it amusing that I ended up in a bank, but that was due to my commerce master's faith in me, not any skills where shorthand and typing was concerned, nor because of any mathematical ability on my part.

My best subjects were English and art. Education didn't seem to be such a major factor in life in those days. More emphasis was given to developing handicraft skills or a trade. Also, just learning to live with people and forming social skills were part of one's education. National military service for young men was compulsory then and at times that interfered with the career of some who had taken up an apprenticeship.

LEARNING TO LIVE WITH PEOPLE AND FORMING
SOCIAL SKILLS WERE PART OF ONE'S OF EDUCATION.

I must have been about twelve years old when I started smoking rolled up newspapers or my mother's dog-ends. By the time my brother married, I was a serious smoker. At his wedding reception I was offered a cigarette. I was just sixteen and, looking at my father, I asked, "Can I have one?"

"Make it the first and the last!" he grunted.

Halfway through smoking it he loudly commented, "You're not smoking that like a novice."

Because Dad seemed so strict and disapproving at times, I felt I had a secret life. I couldn't talk about what I did and could hardly ever bring friends home as I got older. Mum explained years later that Dad had a sister who had "gone off the rails," and he was always afraid that I would do the same. Apparently he never wanted a girl for this reason. Fear for me caused him to be heavy handed at times.

I learned to decorate at an early age. One day while Mum was in hospital with her nerves, Dad said he wanted to redecorate the living-room in the new house before she came home. This was unusual as Dad wasn't a DIY man. He asked me if I would help him. He stripped the walls and we set to doing the wall-papering together in the evening. I found it easier than I realized and Dad went to bed leaving me to finish it around 2:30 in the morning, on my own.

When I left school, my job was with the Midland Bank in the City of London, operating a comptometer, a sort of adding machine/type-writer. Although it was one of the big banks, the office I was in was small with an almost family atmosphere, which I particularly enjoyed. I think I learned about life and how to value and appreciate people from certain older women with whom I worked.

At that time, young women would have a job which they enjoyed, but they didn't expect to return to full-time employment after having children. They would have felt quite fulfilled in the home. There weren't the labor-saving devices in those days and meals were prepared from basic ingredients, taking longer. Most things were homemade in those days. There wasn't so much materialism then either; therefore, there wasn't the financial expectation or pressure. Not having known anything different, I found it all quite acceptable. The home was the center of the family unit and even those more academically qualified than myself didn't seem to expect any other form of lifestyle.

On the whole, in most areas I felt equipped for life although not over confident. In later years when my mother suffered from mental break-downs, it was necessary for me to cope with running the home at quite a young age. I was glad I had been taught and prepared to some extent where this was concerned.

Emotionally though, I wasn't so prepared.

Now the boy Samuel ministered to the Lord before Eli. And the word of the Lord was rare in those days; there was no wide-spread revelation. And it came to pass at that time while Eli was lying down in his place, and when his eyes had begun to grow so dim that he could not see, and before the lamp of God went out in the tabernacle of the Lord where the ark of God was, and while Samuel was lying down, that the Lord called Samuel.

And he answered, "Here I am!" So he ran to Eli and said, "Here am I, for you called me." And he said, "I did not call; lie down again." And he went and lay down. Then the Lord called yet again, "Samuel!" So Samuel arose and went to Eli, and said, "Here I am, for you called me." He answered, "I did not call, my son; lie down again." (Now Samuel did not yet know the Lord, nor was the word of the Lord yet revealed to him.) And the Lord called Samuel again the third time. So he arose and went to Eli, and said, "Here I am, for you did call me." Then Eli perceived that the Lord had called the boy. Therefore Eli said to Samuel, "Go, lie down; and it shall be, if He calls you, that you must say, 'Speak Lord, for Your servant hears.'" So Samuel went and lay down in his place. Now the Lord came and stood and called as at other times, "Samuel! Samuel!" And Samuel answered, "Speak, for Your servant hears" (1 Samuel 3:1-10).

ENDNOTES

1. 1 Corinthians 13:11.

2. 1 Samuel 3:10.

Chapter Five

A Shattered Dream

Remember your Creator before the silver cord is loosed,
Or the golden bowl is broken,
Or the pitcher shattered at the fountain...[1]

THE DREAM

Like most girls approaching womanhood I had boyfriends. I longed for love. I not only believed it would all be different if... I also believed I would be better if I were married, had my own home and eventually had children. I believed these things would make me feel complete as a person and never really knew how to live in the fullness of the present because of the pressing need I felt and the desire I had in achieving these goals. I was looking outside for the answer to the emptiness, the sense of not belonging, and of not fitting in. I didn't realize the missing piece of the jigsaw was inside of me—and was God-shaped.

I DIDN'T REALIZE THE MISSING PIECE OF THE JIGSAW
WAS INSIDE OF ME—AND WAS GOD-SHAPED.

It was of great importance for me to have a current boyfriend; and after a number of romances, I met a young man who I thought was different. He was easy-going and appeared to want my company despite the needs I was aware of in myself. I feared these might be obvious.

Until then, I was so unsure of myself that I was afraid most young men wouldn't want me if they got to know me. I was happy in the fact that this young man got on well with my parents and didn't seem bothered by the simplicity of our lifestyle. I felt more content at home and believed I was in love. After a respectable courtship, we became engaged on my nineteenth birthday, and soon I was planning my dream wedding. Like most girls, I wanted to be married, but for me the desire was from the need for security as well as love.

THE WEDDING

I had been christened a Catholic, but when we went to put the banns[2] up for our wedding in the local Anglican Church, I asked if I could change my religion to Anglican. I felt this would help me to know God and make me feel different. The vicar explained that if I did I would have to agree to attend church once a month. My fiancé objected to this stipulation, so I never pursued it.

I didn't know then that God is not a religion.

I remember the slight feeling of doubt on the morning of my wedding, but thought this was normal and brushed it aside. I've heard since of other brides who have experienced similare feelings. After the wedding, we set up home in the house where I had grown up. The couple who lived downstairs offered us two of the rooms I had lived in as a child which they had never rented out.

But nothing had changed within me. The emptiness was still there.

Having little rent to pay, we were able to work and save hard and, after a couple of years, we bought a house that we could afford, an end terrace in Bexleyheath, Kent. The house needed a lot of work done to it to make it the way we wanted it, which meant responsibility and hard work for us. Although all this brought a sense of achievement and pride, the price to pay was the financial restriction in things like going out for recreation and entertainment. Again, having a home and husband still didn't alter me as a person. I was still as self-centred and insecure, and felt as incomplete as ever.

After a few years, it seemed the time and the appropriate age to consider having a family. With great joy, after a little while, I discovered I was pregnant. This must be it! Love begets love. I would find love at last. The knowledge and anticipation of having this child almost fulfilled all I was looking for.

MOTHERHOOD

When eventually a wonderful baby boy was placed in my arms, I didn't know whether to laugh or cry. For the first time in my life I felt I had someone who belonged to me. But as the weeks and months went by after Matthew's birth, I became more aware of my own great need and a desperate loneliness and inadequacy. This little child I loved needed me and I wondered what I had to offer him. I continued to work in the City of London for as long as I could, until just before he was born. Whereas I had a few friendships, we hadn't lived in Bexleyheath long so hadn't made friends there. I now missed companionship very much. My own family members were in such emotional need, and I didn't have a good relationship with my in-laws, which was mainly due to my own jealousy where my mother-in-law was concerned. She could do nothing right in my eyes. As she once said, if she had said the floor was white, I would have said it was black. She was right. I knew this, but couldn't do a thing about it. It was just me.

I tried to look beyond myself and my own emptiness to my husband, but he suddenly seemed like a stranger to me. We appeared to have nothing in common apart from parenthood. Beyond him, there were relations we seldom saw and whose lives weren't part of ours.

My prison was now like solitary confinement. Still nothing had changed inside me. It had, in fact, only become worse. The present seemed lonely and empty, and the future suddenly looked frighteningly bleak.

THE CRY OF MY HEART

Matthew was asleep in the lounge and I was in the kitchen, when I remember a cry came from within my heart, "Oh God, this is my life!" I was thinking of this little child I had brought into a world where every relationship was strained. I loved him but what life could I offer him?

A SENSE OF GUILT AND RESPONSIBILITY ENGULFED ME,
COUPLED WITH THE LONGING TO FEEL I BELONGED.

It must all be my fault. A sense of guilt and responsibility engulfed me, coupled with the longing to feel I belonged. A compelling force came over me to change things and make myself different. With my will, I would love my husband, my family, and my in-laws.

I became aware that my vision appeared blurred. I saw the doctor about making an appointment with an optician. He must have suspected something as he said, "The answer will be a lemon! Come back and see me." I didn't know this was an indication of something else to him. He was right, there was nothing wrong with my eyes.

THE BREAKDOWN

Soon this condition developed into a state where I could no longer cope from day to day. I was crying continually and not eating or sleeping at night. This lasted at least three weeks. I struggled to look after Matthew and while he slept during the day I would pull a blanket over myself, curl up and sleep on the couch. Everything seemed unreal. I felt alone and frightened.

I had always blamed my mother-in-law for our poor relationship. Now I suddenly realized how at fault I had been and became almost obsessed to get on with her. As I now tried to love her, in a strange sort of way she no longer seemed the problem. I was!

One of the neighbors who lived across the road came to see me; she must have heard I was in distress. She was so kind and started visiting me and would take my laundry. While she was with me on one occasion, she told me she was a Christian and how Jesus helped her and what her faith meant to her. Although I believed her, I couldn't connect what she was saying with my own plight. One afternoon she took Matthew and me to a mother and toddler group run by her church. At the end of the afternoon, the young women stood in a circle and prayed. I stood in the circle, but I felt out of place and on the outside of what was happening, and wished I were part of this.

When Matthew's first birthday arrived, instead of enjoying it I felt unable to celebrate or even know what to do. My neighbor seemed so understanding. She had Matthew and me over, bought a simple cake, put a candle on it and made a little birthday tea party with her own children. While I was in her house, a psychiatrist arrived; my doctor had sent for him. When he saw the state I was in, he insisted that I should be admitted to his ward in the local hospital.

Devastated and desperate, I had no choice.

Somehow I must have gathered together the things I needed for hospital; but when it came to leaving my Matthew, it was an agony, which ripped me apart inside.

All I can remember was being driven away on my little son's first birthday, clutching his baby photographs, screaming, "Don't take me away from my baby!"

My dream had fallen apart.

So had I.

Can a woman forget her nursing child, and not have compassion on the son of her womb? Surely they may forget, yet I will not forget you (Isaiah 49:15).

ENDNOTES

1. Ecclesiastes 12:6.

2. The banns of marriage or, simply "the banns," (from an Old English word meaning "to summon") are the public announcement from the pulpit that a marriage is going to take place in that church between two specified persons at a specified time. http://www.wordiq.com/definition/Banns; accessed December 28, 2010.

Chapter Six

The Beginning of the End

Forever beginning what never shall end!
–The Wesley Brothers

In the hospital I tried to find somewhere in the lounge where I could curl up under a blanket as I had done before at home. When my husband came to visit me he seemed to find this amusing, referring to the cartoon character Linus, who always carried a blanket with him. I felt far from a source of amusement.

Returning home from the brief period of treatment, I felt patched up, better, but strange. I remembered experiencing similar feelings as a child—of unreality, and imagined what happened to me had somehow caused me to revert back to the person I was then. I feared life could never be the same again. In this unsettled state, I coped by keeping myself busy but, back in the familiar circumstances and left alone with my thoughts, I began to cry again. If anyone asked how I was, I would burst into tears and I didn't know why.

My doctor was very supportive. I confided in him, "I don't have the confidence to talk to the doctor I saw before."

"I'll find someone you will like."

Soon I was given an appointment at a private clinic at Guy's hospital in London. This was an exclusive clinic and I felt privileged.

I confessed to the consultant, "I can't face the future with my husband and I can't face it without him."

He asked, "Do you feel desperate?" When I said yes, he arranged for me to be admitted into his clinic immediately.

THE YORK CLINIC

During the six weeks I spent in the York Clinic, I received every attention, plus fellow patients who not only understood how I felt but seemed to appreciate that I understood them. The company and kind surroundings gave me comfort and security. Of course this was a diversion from my problem and an escape. The treatment in the clinic was mainly talking, and at the start I found this difficult. One night I was told I was to be kept awake all night, the night staff would help me. The night seemed long, lonely, and boring, just one nurse and me. They gave me a game of solitaire with glass marbles to pass the time. I remember how each move sounded so loud in the silence of the darkened ward. I wondered what to expect in the morning.

A registrar, junior doctor, arrived the next day. I was lying on a couch in a consulting room, covered with a red rug. He gave me an injection. A nurse sat at my feet. The young doctor began to talk quietly to me, asking me questions. I was in a semi-conscious state and the bed appeared to have reversed direction. Whatever drug I was given took away any inhibitions. Until then I had not been able to talk about my thoughts and fears. Now I spoke quite freely.

UNTIL THEN I HAD NOT BEEN ABLE TO TALK ABOUT
MY THOUGHTS AND FEARS. NOW I SPOKE QUITE FREELY.

The young registrar asked about my marriage and my life in general. I confessed the lack of feelings I now realized I had for my husband and the way I felt toward my mother-in-law. I talked about my own parents and of the family who used to live below us that I saw as a model family.

He asked me who I did have feelings for, and I said for him. When he asked why, I told him it was because of how he had spoken to me.

On waking, and when my memory returned, I was extremely distraught at all I had shared and was distressed that I had admitted to my fears, feelings, and emotions. I was helped into bed by the ward sister. Later when he came to see me, I was inconsolable.

"Don't you feel better now all that is out?" he gently asked.

But my fears about my circumstances and the future seemed to magnify. They were suddenly unbearable. The rest of the six weeks were spent discussing my past, the things that had lingered in my memory and the present fears that gave way to dread of the future. In time, I did find a release in talking and learned to deal with suppressed thoughts. But the comfort of being in the clinic was suddenly dispelled when I was told I was to be sent home for the weekend on a pass to see how I would cope. I was confused in the light of the conversations about where my life, marriage, and feelings were concerned. I found the prospect of going home daunting.

RETURN TO REALITY

It's difficult to describe how I felt when I got home, trying to marry up things that had been said to me with reality. I endeavored to be as normal as I knew how. Matthew was still being cared for by an aunt of my husband, so I didn't have him to look after. I tried to take on everyday chores, but there was a strange sense of not belonging. I was aware of a feeling of not being married, which I later described to the doctor. The home didn't have the interest or meaning it formerly had, and my mind kept churning over the thoughts that invaded it. I tried to analyze and come to terms with them, as I had been taught. Television was a new acquisition in our home; it was the year of the World Cup which, surprisingly, I found vaguely interesting.

One evening while the television was on, I was distracted by my thoughts, when my husband suddenly asked, "What are you thinking about?"

"The things I've been told to think about."

"Anything except the baby and me," he flung at me.

Although this was true in a sense, he was unable to understand, and an enormous argument broke out. We argued about how the situation of my being hospitalized had come about. He couldn't see why I didn't feel able to carry on as I once did.

I was reminded of things I had said, "You always said you were happy."

I began to feel guilty that I had become ill.

"I think you have been holding a candle for the chap you met in the Isle of Wight," he said. This was someone I had met years before and I had difficulty forgetting.

I felt helpless and defenseless and, for me, this was the worst thing that could happen. We weren't on the phone at that time, so before I knew it, I found myself running from the house to a nearby phone box. I knew I couldn't stay. I phoned the only person I felt I could turn to. Beryl, a friend from childhood lived within walking distance. We grew up in the same house and, if I'm honest, she was one of the reasons for choosing to live in Bexleyheath.

Beryl realized I was distressed and things were serious when I explained what had happened and how I felt. "You'd better come round," she offered.

Going back into the house, I simply collected a nightdress and toothbrush. The atmosphere was still heated, and my husband tried to demand my key from me before I ran out again.

That was the end of my marriage!

It was about 11 at night and a considerable walk to Roy and Beryl's home, but I didn't give that a thought. A feeling of desperation propelled me. In their home I slept on a make-shift bed in the livingroom. In the morning, Roy phoned the clinic and was told to send me back to them.

A FEELING OF DESPERATION PROPELLED ME.

When Beryl said, "I couldn't sleep for fear of what you might have done during the night," I realized the position I must have put them in.

Returning briefly that morning to my house for some clothes, I found it empty. Fortunately my husband had left for work. After packing a suitcase, I caught a train and made my way to the clinic. On arrival, I saw a social worker who then phoned my parents. They were asked to look after me and I was even more confused by the conversation. They must have been unprepared, and I could tell they were reluctant to take me, but were told my time at the clinic had come to an end. When they agreed, the social worker drove me to their home.

MY PARENTS' HOME

My parents must have found that period as difficult as I did. Others have found after leaving home, it is not easy to return. But I was grateful to them and felt almost obliged.

It wasn't long before Matthew was brought to see me. In the semi-security of my parents' home I could enjoy seeing him, observed changes in him, and realized that I wanted him with me. My parents agreed that he should come and live with me at their home. This was soon arranged.

It was good to have him back. I concentrated on trying to make him feel secure and occupied. This was good for me. Life had purpose again. Mum and Dad were quite supportive and, I believe, did their best for us both.

Not knowing where my life was going, I seemed to be treading water, time-wise. I was still attending the clinic and seeing the young doctor who had overseen my case throughout. He never seemed to be surprised by any turn of events, and we both knew I was very dependent on my visits.

I had long realized the attachment I had formed and imagined it wasn't discouraged. By the nature of his questions, I began to feel there was an expectation for me to move on. But where? I scanned the newspapers for a flat of some sort that I could afford on the little money I received from the state and within reach of my parents. They suddenly seemed all I had, apart from Mike, my cousin. He had visited me in hospital and shown a deep interest and care for me. When I found a semi-basement bedsitter in Bromley, Kent, for Matthew and me, Mike helped move our few belongings.

ALONE, AS A SINGLE MOTHER

The room I rented was large with adequate furniture but no running water. It was dimly lit as its bay window was half below ground. Eye level was ground level. It was off a corridor that led to other flats or rooms. The bathroom was shared. There was a single bed in our room and, as Matthew was still sleeping in his cot, I put this in the corner between the bed and the wall. After Matthew was in bed at night I would sit in the dim light of a table lamp so as not to wake him. There was no television, but I would listen to a little radio and knit or write letters, many of which were to the doctor at the clinic. I also received letters from him. I was finding the weaning process difficult as my appointments were becoming fewer.

The room had a small electric cooker in the corner on which I tried to make interesting meals for us both. In those days there wasn't all the support for single mothers that became available in later years, such as housing benefits. There were some advantages where we lived such as launderettes for our washing and a large park nearby that we often visited. However, this soon became a prison of a different kind. In one sense I was free to do my own thing...but what was that? Alone with a small child in one room, I soon learned the total commitment of being a single parent twenty-four hours a day!

IN ONE SENSE I WAS FREE TO DO MY OWN THING... BUT WHAT WAS THAT?

My husband visited Matthew one afternoon a week. His job only allowed him that amount of time off. He would come and take him out; these visits for me were a respite or reprieve from responsibility for a few hours. My cousin, Mike, lived on the other side of London but would drive over each Sunday and take us out—or sometimes just Matthew for a game of ball in the park. Mike was a scientist and was a serious, studious, reliable person. Although he was a bachelor, he was good with Matthew, who loved him. Matthew would ask if "Bike" was coming, as he called him. Being alone, I lived for Mike's visits in many ways. But he too became a crutch.

Matthew was a healthy active normal little boy who needed attention and recreation like all children. I found myself very preoccupied with my lot and the uncertainties of the future. I had told the consultant that I couldn't live with or without my husband. Now I was without him, having no real home and no confidence to get a job, even if I had help in caring for Matthew. The reality that Matthew would need a father as well as a mother as he grew up made me feel extremely inadequate and quite afraid. I found no inner strength when I needed to be firm with him, instead there was the fear of losing his love. Again it became difficult to live in the present because of the insecurity of the seemingly impossible future.

A young couple, who lived along the corridor in a bed-sitter with a separate kitchen moved out. I took their rooms, which made it easier during the evenings when Matthew was asleep in the bedroom.

We would go out as much as possible, often to the park where there were tame squirrels to feed. Another park had a small pool where Matthew sailed his little yacht. From the bridge over the nearby railway line, we could watch the trains come and go and wave to the drivers, who always responded. I travelled to my parents' home once a week, also to Beryl's. Beryl had two small children who were good for Matthew to play with, and I valued these visits. She was extremely kind to us.

But these days would end in long, lonely evenings and solitary nights for me.

Being a single mother I needed patience to bring Matthew up, and teach him things he needed to be encouraged in. The responsibility seemed such a strain. I didn't know how to put him first when my own need was so great. A child demands so much mental energy, which I didn't have. Chinks began to appear in my self-made sanity, which made coping all the more difficult.

CHINKS BEGAN TO APPEAR IN MY SELF-MADE SANITY,
WHICH MADE COPING ALL THE MORE DIFFICULT.

The outside door we used was on a Yale lock which unlatched from the inside. Matthew learned how to climb up and unlock it and let himself out. On these occasions, I would have to chase after him. I couldn't secure the door as other people had to use it. At times he would have reached the little park next to the house by the time I noticed he was gone and went to find to him. This became a real problem for me. I noticed signs that worried me about Matthew and mentioned this to our doctor. At times he would throw his toys for no apparent reason. I also found toilet training difficult and it worried me that he wasn't out of nappies yet. All this began to prey on my mind, which accentuated the problems.

Our doctor referred him to a pediatrician who assured me, "There is nothing wrong with Matthew." But added, "It's you!"

That seemed like a death blow—and what had I dreaded hearing. Soon our doctor was arranging for me to see a psychiatric doctor in a nearby hospital. This familiar pattern filled me with dread. Everything I had fought and feared for Matthew was coming to pass. The memory of my own mother in and out of mental hospitals haunted me. Now I was to be admitted into a hospital for the third time in almost as many years. We had only been in these rooms for about a year, and Matthew was not yet three years of age.

To be responsible for one's own life is one thing. To be responsible for another's, especially one so dependent, when in such desperate need, is a greater burden. How could I make a life for my son and me when life seemed pointless? Even worse, Matthew had become my reason for living. Had it not been for him, I wouldn't have wanted to get up in the morning. My life was going nowhere; what future was there for him with just me? How could I make life seem meaningful for him?

THE DECISION

Our doctor said that I was to be admitted into a nearby hospital. The prospect of this was grim. Even more grim was the effect that all this could have on Matthew.

I faced myself and I faced my life.

As my husband had said, "This can't go on." I felt it couldn't go on but what was the alternative? There was no prospect of a life for Matthew with me. The situation was deteriorating, not improving. I knew that and the hopelessness of my circumstances was an agony. I loved Matthew too much to ruin his life, but I couldn't see what I could do. His father loved him too. And as much as I didn't want to admit it, it was obvious that Matthew would be better off with him. It was Matthew's life or mine.

I knew what I had to do, but could I do it? I tried to crucify my own feelings to make the choice. I had to make the cold-blooded decision alone.

Matthew should go to his father to be brought up by him! He was young enough to adjust. The doctor had reassured me that he was too young for all this to affect him permanently. If I put it off any longer, it would all take its toll on Matthew. No mother wants to be forgotten, but I didn't want to be a mother one minute and not there the next. Neither did I want to be a mother he visited—a tug of love kind of life. If I couldn't be a mother in the fullest sense, I couldn't bear to be one in part.

Even though it would feel like the end for me, somehow I had to walk out of his life. I had to give him up. I told his father of my decision. What became of me after that didn't seem important.

We planned for him to collect Matthew.

Steeling myself for the ordeal, I packed my son's clothes. He didn't have so many really...the little red leather boots he was so proud of, the blue dressing gown with the lady-bird buttons, and his pyjamas which were too small, as were other things. Coping to buy these had become a problem for me. He wasn't going to need his cot, but I gathered together the toys that he played with most. Among these was his teddy bear.

As arranged, his father arrived to take Matthew away.

The moment had come. Matthew's few belongings were handed over in silence. Then I picked him up and held my little son for the last time. Looking at him, I said goodbye more with my heart than my lips as I lifted him into his father's arms.

Then they were gone.

BITTERSWEET PEACE

The dreadful sense of loss tore me inside, but I didn't cry. The feelings were of inevitability. I knew I had to give him up. It wasn't just because I couldn't cope or give him a life with me. There was something beyond myself that gave me the strength to let him go. It was as if I had to do it. I didn't consciously think of God; but somewhere within me I felt only God knew, and there was a bittersweet sort of peace that came over me. I knew what I was doing was for Matthew's good.

...ONE NAME CAME INTO MY HEART, JESUS.

Strangely enough as I handed Matthew to his father, one name came into my heart, Jesus. I didn't know why and paid no attention to it.

Looking back, perhaps I wasn't alone after all.

A hymn I learned and mention much later summed it up.

Matthew was taken to be cared for this time by Barbara, my sister-in-law, who lived in the same house where my in-laws lived. He was settling down and played with the children in the garden happily, I was told. It was suggested that I could observe him from a distance. The house was a few doors in from a corner. From the road beside the houses I could overlook the garden. It was arranged; Barbara took me to where I could see him and as I watched him I was unsure what I was looking for. Afraid that he would see me, yet strangely wishing he would, I drew away. Barbara slipped her arm around my shoulders as I bit back the tears. We walked away in silence.

I felt helpless and numb.

He was there and my arms longed to hold him.

That was the last I saw of him…then.

> …*Then she* [Hagar] *departed and wandered in the Wilderness of Beersheba. And the water in the skin was used up, and she placed the boy under one of the shrubs. Then she went and sat down across from him at a distance of about a bowshot; for she said to herself, "Let me not see the death of the boy." So she sat opposite him, and lifted up her voice and wept* (Genesis 21:14-16).

Chapter Seven

The End of the Beginning

Behold I stand at the door and knock (Revelation 3:20).

THE SENTENCE

Alone, like someone beginning a prison sentence, I was admitted into the local hospital. Deep down I thought I'd be there for the rest of my life. I remember saying to Mike, "It feels like the beginning of the end."

His reply surprised me, "You mean the end of the beginning." I didn't know then he was quoting Winston Churchill or what significance there was in that remark. There seemed nothing to me that could begin in the future. There was nothing but an empty desolation inside me.

The rooms that I rented were left with my belongings in them but I really felt quite homeless. Going into hospital, I thought, would solve the problem of my own position and state; and if I submitted myself into their hands, they'd find an answer. After a little while in hospital though, the subject of discharge was brought up. This caused me to panic, as I hadn't anticipated that. It made me realize no one knew the dreadful condition I was really in.

It jolted me into reality.

In my tortured mind, I had imagined a life consigned to a mental institution of some kind for the rest of my days. The only comfort I felt was in knowing Matthew was being cared for and, hopefully, stood a chance of stability. To others, I was a young woman responsible for my own life. In fact some thought I had everything to live for! All I was aware of was that my marriage had gone, my mental health had gone, and my little son had gone. The past was a mess, the present unbearable, and the future terrifying. I couldn't see any reason to live, and had no desire to continue. In fact, I felt as if I didn't deserve to live, but none of us can just stop being. The only alternative began to form as a plan in my mind. I must end my life!

I FELT AS IF I DIDN'T DESERVE TO LIVE,
BUT NONE OF US CAN JUST STOP BEING.

This was no cry for help. This was for real.

THE OPEN DOOR

I was in an open ward where patients could come and go. It wasn't difficult to plan how to go about things. I excused myself, walked out of the hospital, and made my way to my flat. I collected boxes of aspirins from chemist to chemist on the way, as they were sold only in small quantities. I also asked for change to ensure the gas meter would be full. My mother-in-law worked in a family member's greengrocer's shop nearby. I stopped off. I had been very jealous of her over the years and had opposed her continually, causing trouble. For the first time, I recognized my own responsibility in this relationship and I suddenly had a great desire to put things right.

I SUDDENLY HAD A GREAT DESIRE TO PUT THINGS RIGHT.

Going into the shop, I called her to one side, "I'm sorry for everything and how I've been."

She looked embarrassed and uncomfortable, "It was as much my fault." She said, excusing herself saying she was needed to serve.

Feeling satisfied, I made my way purposefully until I reached the flat. There was a determination about me. I hadn't planned to leave any note. Letters I had received from the young registrar that could have been misunderstood if found I had sent to Mike, asking him to destroy them. I couldn't.

From memory I would have said I had bought hundreds of soluble aspirins. There certainly was an extremely large quantity. I emptied these into several cups and filled them with water. Having everything ready, one by one I took them all. Going into the dingy bed-sitter I put myself to bed, hoping that I would just not wake up again. Instead, after a few minutes I was violently sick!

I then filled the gas meter, picked up a pillow, went into the kitchen, and placed it in the bottom of the oven.

But then came the fear of the result should I succeed. Just what would death hold for me? Because of what I had been taught in Sunday school, I believed in God. Or I certainly hoped in God. Therefore I knew that I would surely meet Him if I died, as we all must. It wasn't so much the prospect of dying but of facing God, knowing that He knew all about me, that filled me with a deep fear. Anticipating His gaze, I realized I had been to blame for so much that had happened. I also didn't like the person I had become.

I remember thinking, *If I could pin this on someone else I would.* But I couldn't. I, alone, was the offender. In this I took the death sentence and mentally carried it out. God convicted me, but I had to strike the death blow to the self who had sinned. Having done so, all that was left for me was to abandon myself to His mercy and grace and thus His absolute pardon.

BEFORE GOD, WE STAND ALONE.

Before God, we stand alone. We can blame our past, our circumstances, or our parents, but at the end of the day we are responsible for our own life and condition.

The only path that seemed open for me was to terminate my life. And, although this appeared the only solution, with the awful weight of guilt came the desire and longing to be able to say I'm sorry to God before I did.

THE ENCOUNTER

I knew nothing about repentance, as the Bible calls it, and as Jesus requires. But with the oven door open beside me and a pillow in the bottom, I cried from my heart, "O God, I'm sorry for my life!"

My eyes saw nothing. There was no flash of light. But it was as if the sky had opened and I knew my spirit had made contact with Him. I had met the God of Heaven Himself, and in that moment felt His forgiveness—and Heaven poured into my heart.

I MET THE GOD OF HEAVEN HIMSELF, AND IN THAT MOMENT
FELT HIS FORGIVENESS—AND HEAVEN POURED INTO MY HEART.

Suddenly I felt assured that God knew everything and understood why I had to give up Matthew. If no one else on the face of the earth knew, I knew God knew.

In that moment, God had become my God.

Joy and an enormous sense of gratitude overwhelmed me. God had removed the weight and unbearable guilt of my past, my condition, and my sin. The balm of His forgiveness flooded my soul and soothed the pain. The indescribable sense of His presence pervaded my being with a wonderful love.

I was free. I was clean.

I didn't really understand what had happened to me. My circumstances were unchanged and my mind still in turmoil, but there was an incredible peace within me. I no longer feared meeting God. His acceptance of my penitence transmitted His righteousness, in response, to my heart. I no longer feared judgment.

One encounter with Jesus changed my soul forever.

I little knew then that God had entered my life, Himself.

THE ATTEMPT

Not realizing exactly what all this meant, I still saw no other way left. Staring at the open oven door, it seemed the only course open to me. Fearlessly but reluctantly, turning the gas tap on full, I laid my head on the pillow.

How long would it take? What would I feel?

There was a fear of the unknown and a feeling of finality and aloneness.

I don't recall any unpleasant smell or being aware of becoming unconscious. But as I drifted in and out of consciousness I would come to and find myself lying on the floor on the opposite side of the kitchen not knowing how I got there!

Crawling back, I put my head on the pillow, only to come round on the other side of the kitchen again.

How had I got there? There was no natural answer.

The next thing I recall was the kindly Polish landlady standing over me and telling someone to open the window. I was coming to on the floor. Soon my head was cradled in an ambulance man's arms as I was being driven back to hospital. He was asking me questions as to all that I had done. Trying to comfort me, he assured me that he had tried to do something similar. In hospital, there were more questions. I found myself in an intensive care unit to start with where I was treated in a matter-of-fact manner from some and with indifference from a few others.

REALIZATION

Later, after I recovered and was back in the main ward, I felt somehow different. I was aware of a great love and compassion for other patients as I mixed with them. I wanted to pray, but didn't really know how.

Verses of Scripture, which I must have learned as a child, kept coming into my mind. The Bible says, "The Holy Spirit will bring to your remembrance all things that I said to you."[1] Perhaps that's why looking at fellow patients I found myself repeating the verse, "Judge not that you are not judged."[2] When someone commented that I was good, Jesus' words, "There is none good but God" came to me.[3]

As I considered my parents and grandparents, then Matthew, verses about, "The sins of the parents to the third and fourth generation,"[4] made me hope that would stop with me! As I was trying to help with some dishes in the kitchen, I made a mistake and sensed hostility from some patients. I found my reaction was to turn my heart to God and quote Jesus' prayer, "Father, forgive them."[5]

It is impossible to describe exactly what happened to me. It was as if a vision or impression of the cross, with Jesus on it, embraced my spirit and I was released toward God, while part seemed to separate from me. There was an awareness of a demonic presence that fled from me.

THE CHANGE

After this, I felt I was in another realm. It is best described by Scripture, "It is no longer I who lives, but Christ lives in me."[6] The hospital might still have seemed a prison, but it now no longer had bars. I was free within myself to do things I would have hated doing before. The routine was an opportunity to show willingness. Other patients were people to love, and I now wanted to serve them. Jesus was real to me and was with me in the hospital. I discovered an enabling He was giving me, a strength not my own. The sense of pointlessness had gone.

"JESUS, I ONLY WANT TO DO WHAT YOU WANT ME
TO DO AND GO WHERE YOU WANT ME TO GO."

I began to wonder what I could do with the future and found myself praying, "Jesus, I only want to do what You want me to do and go where You want me to go," adding, "I'll even do housework if it's for You." Until then I had hated housework! My life was changing on the inside. My attitude was changing, especially toward others. It's really all about meeting Jesus. Only He can come into the inside and change us. There was an innocent ignorance as to what had happened to me. I later realized that this was, in fact, the baptism in the Holy Spirit.

Much later I discovered how miraculous was the preservation from what I had attempted to do. The house where I had lived was made into bed sits or small flat-lets. These were rented by people who mostly were out working during the day. On this day, a man who lived in one of these rooms along the corridor, whom I didn't know, came home from work unexpectedly. His job was manual and had been abandoned that day because of the weather. He smelled gas when he came into the house, investigated, and found me.

Despite my attempt, God had stepped in.

I have heard of You by the hearing of the ear, but now my eyes see You. Therefore I abhor myself, and repent in dust and ashes (Job 42:4-6).

ENDNOTES

1. See John 14:26.

2. Matthew 7:1.

3. See Romans 3:11.

4. See Deuteronomy 5:9.

5. Luke 23:34.

6. Galatians 2:20.

The Love that Found Me

When from womb my life began
To spiral on its downward way
There was no help could come from man
To lift my feet from out of clay.
T'was Adam, nay, perhaps t'was Eve
That set the course for me to run,
And from the outset they held sway
To their nature I'd willingly succumb.
But lo, before their day was born
Another saw my plight and pain
And in His love a plan did form
That would, by blood, my own life gain.
I didn't see His birth or death.
In blindness made my way until
There was nothing left on earth
That could undo what was my will.
Then from a feeble hope that He,
Before death sealed me for Eternity,
Would ease the lonely agony
And hear my sorrowful plea.
"I'm sorry God." was all I called,
But that was all it took to make
The door of Heaven open wide
And my inner hell-born nature shake.
When His blood bought pardon was applied
Himself, He came. He'd waited long,
To accomplish what He longed to do,
Set me free to Him belong.

Chapter Eight

The Start of My Search

I once was lost but now I'm found,
Was blind but now I see.
–John Newton, Amazing Grace

THE INTRODUCTION

While I was in hospital, my cousin Mike visited as often as he could. Routine in there continued, but for me things were now different. There was a new dimension to my life. My spirit was alive in a way it had never been before, but the fact was I didn't really know what had happened. All I knew was Heaven was within me, Jesus was real, and all I could think about was God. I didn't want to lose this state and re-member thinking that the only person who never displeased God was Jesus. If I got to know Him and followed Him, I'd be all right.

Mike was a scientist and I thought he had the answer to everything. I tried to explain what had happened to me, but he just looked puzzled when I talked about my thoughts and what I was experiencing.

"This is like what Tony is saying to me," he said. Tony was his flat mate who had also suffered from depression and had recently become a Christian. "Tony says he talks to God!"

Mike invited me to go and stay for the weekend in North London, where he lived. Tony was away for the weekend. I went, and while there he suggested that we went to visit someone. It was the last thing I felt like doing, especially not knowing who it was, but for Mike's sake, or so I thought, I went. When we got to this young couple's home, we talked for a while when suddenly Chris, the husband, said, "Why have you come?" This sounded very odd and not very friendly to me.

Mike replied, "You helped Tony, so I wondered if you could help Jean."

Chris and Marian apparently were the couple who had led Tony to Christ. Realizing this couple were genuine, I began to explain the turmoil in my mind, the inexplicable things that were happening, and my sudden awareness of God. Chris didn't seem at all surprised. Instead he said, "This is spiritual."

I BEGAN TO EXPLAIN THE TURMOIL IN MY MIND, THE INEXPLICABLE THINGS THAT WERE HAPPENING, AND MY SUDDEN AWARENESS OF GOD.

While talking to me, he testified, "I have Jesus living inside me."

What a thing to say! I thought this was some kind of heresy.

"I have friends more experienced in these things than myself. Bring Jean back next week and I'll invite them."

The following week I met Dave, Andy, and Ken. I found these fine young men easy to talk to and felt at ease; they seemed able to grasp what I was trying to say. They said they wanted time to pray and asked Mike to bring me the following week.

When we met again, they asked what had been happening in my life. I told them my inner thoughts about God and of a conflict I was experiencing, "When I try to do something right, I find there is a hindrance—yet when not trying, there is an ease and ability."

"We want to pray with you and for you," they said.

I agreed, and they gathered round me.

They prayed in a gentle authoritative way, then began to pray in what seemed to be a foreign language. I didn't know what it was but remember a great sense of peace and calm while they did so. One of them,

I believe it was Andy, invited me to follow him in a prayer. On looking back, it could have been what is often referred to as the sinner's prayer.

When they talked to me about God, they used the name "Lord" with familiarity. Soon they were talking to me about my circumstances and future. They asked many questions, and showed concern that I was in a mental hospital, and that my only alternative was to go back to my empty flat.

They spoke of my discharge from hospital, "There are places where we can arrange for you to stay; houses you can go to live in for an unlimited period of time. One house is in Exeter and another is in Liverpool."

For some inexplicable reason I said, "Exeter!" I remember around that time I had prayed, "I only want to do what You want me to do and go where You want me to go," feeling the need of security in doing what God wanted.

Sitting beside me on the couch holding my hand, Mike exclaimed, "Liverpool is nearer!"

This didn't seem important to me; Exeter it was.

I hadn't realized how all this was affecting Mike.

MY FIRST FELLOWSHIP MEETING

We had met in Chris and Marian's home during this time. The next time we met was on a Sunday morning in Reading, where Mike took me for the day. We were in the home of Dave and Yvonne. There we met Ken's wife, Barbara, and Andy's wife, Margie. Going into the living room, I noticed there were two hymn books placed on each seat. Neither of them looked familiar to me. When we were all seated, the women took out scarves and slipped them on their heads, which was obviously their custom. I later learned what it says in Scripture regarding head covering. I remember thinking, I want this.

The natural, simple, yet meaningful manner of these young couples spoke of something I knew I was looking for. Everything seemed new, vital, and there was an awakening within me. Suddenly my life was taking on meaning, perhaps for the first time. I don't remember exactly what took place during that meeting, but from gatherings of this kind over the years since, it would have included an open time of prayer, hymns chosen by those present, sharing from Scripture, and the reality of the risen Christ in His people's lives.

These three couples all went on to be leaders of large Fellowships which, at the time of this writing, are still going strong.

IT'S A WONDERFUL FEELING TO FEEL FOUND! NOT JUST TO
FIND SOMEONE BUT TO FEEL FOUND AFTER FEELING SO LOST.

In the familiar hymn we sing, "I once was lost but now I'm found...." It's a wonderful feeling to feel found! Not just to find someone but to feel found after feeling so lost. The hymn says, "Was blind but now I see...." Only the pure in heart see God, and until we have our hearts cleansed, we can't see properly, even our reasoning isn't clear.

Seated round the table in Dave and Yvonne's dining room afterward, we shared a fondue meal. At the end of the meal, Dave made a phone call to a man respectfully called Mr. North. I later learned that he was a man of God, who God had used in preaching, teaching, personal counsel, and encouragement in the building of many Fellowships throughout the UK. Phone calls were being made and arrangements under way for me to go to Exeter. My discharge from hospital was also obtained. Mr. and Mrs. North lived in the house adjacent to the one where I was to go and live. Dave asked if I'd like to speak to him.

"Is there anything you'd like to ask?" the warm and friendly voice on the phone asked me. Thinking only practically, I replied, "Do I have to bring my own linen?"

"No Lovie, everything will be provided." This amuses me now because I still don't know what he gathered from my question but later Dave told me Mr. North said, "She wants God."

The next time we spoke was when I met Mr. North in Exeter. I'm glad, like God, he had read my heart.

So it was that God removed me from the mental hospital and placed me in a home of His choice. His word says, "He sets the solitary in families" (Ps. 68:6).

O Lord, You have searched me and known me, You know my sitting down and my rising up; You understand my thought afar off. You comprehend my path and my lying down, and are acquainted with all my ways. For there is not a word on my tongue, but behold, O Lord, You know it altogether. You have hedged me behind and before, and laid Your hand upon me. Such knowledge is too wonderful for me; it is high, I cannot attain it. Where can I go from Your Spirit? Or where can I flee from Your presence? If I ascend into heaven You are there;...if I take the wings of the morning, and dwell in the uttermost parts of the sea, even there Your hand shall lead me, and Your right hand shall hold me. If I say, "Surely the darkness shall fall on me," even the night shall be light about me; indeed the darkness shall not hide from You, but the night shines as the day; the darkness and the light are both alike to You. For You formed my inward parts; You covered me in my mother's womb. I will praise You, for I am fearfully and wonderfully made; marvelous are Your works, and that my soul knows very well. My frame was not hidden from You, when I was made in secret, and skillfully wrought in the lowest parts of the earth. Your eyes saw my substance, being yet unformed. And in Your book they all were written, the days fashioned for me, when as yet there were none of them. How precious also are Your thoughts to me, O God! How great is the sum of them! If I should count them, they would be more in number than the sand; When I awake I am still with You.... Search me O God, and know my heart; try me and know my anxieties; and see if there is any wicked way in me, and lead me in the way everlasting (Psalm 139).

Jean at 17

Last picture taken of
Matthew as a child

Matthew and Jean
after their reunion

Chapter Nine

Not Knowing Whither

God holds the key to all unknown,
And I am glad.
If other hands should hold the key,
Or if He trusted it to me,
I would be sad.[1]

THE JOURNEY

It was time to leave London. My discharge was obtained from hospital and arrangements had been made for me to go to Exeter, neither of which I had anything to do with. In my bag were my train ticket that Mike had bought and the sandwiches he had packed for the journey. En route to the station, we stopped at a bookshop to buy a Bible. He said I would need one. How did he know that? We didn't know there were so many versions and how to choose one, but we soon left with a simple Bible in a paper bag.

Packing for the future hadn't been easy as I little knew what to expect, except that my life was going to be very different. I welcomed the change. Already I found my taste in clothes had altered, some I just didn't want to take. Other things had lost their appeal. I had always worn a considerable amount of makeup and was extremely fashionable and fussy with my hair. These things no longer seemed important. For the first time, I enjoyed the feeling of freedom in washing my face, combing my hair and not having to bother with makeup. To many, these outward expressions of my life would not have seemed wrong, but for me they smacked of the old and all I no longer wanted. I didn't just want to be free inside but also wanted my life simpler and more real. I was a heavy smoker. I now didn't want to smoke any more. I had managed to cut down quite a bit but hadn't quite got the victory.

I DIDN'T JUST WANT TO BE FREE INSIDE BUT ALSO
WANTED MY LIFE SIMPLER AND MORE REAL.

It was time to make my way South. Before I boarded the train, Mike and I said goodbye on the platform. I had a feeling of well-being but sadness that Mike couldn't enter into what was happening. As we looked at each other, we both recognized that life wasn't to be the same for either of us in the future. It wasn't just the distance. I knew he had misgivings that I was going to be such a long way from him. I thanked him for everything.

"I'll phone soon and drive down to see you," Mike said. "Ask the couple who run the house if I can stay. I'll take you onto the moors." He looked quite forlorn, concerned, and resigned as I took my place in the train. I watched him as the train pulled out of the station. Mike looked alone.

As I settled down on my own, I had to stop myself thinking of him. I wondered who would come to meet me. How would we recognize each other?

There is no striking memory of the journey. I opened the paper bag, took out my new Bible, and starting at Genesis. I'll read it like a story book, I thought. I didn't even know there was a New and Old Testament! It was hard going and my concentration was so poor. I was also aware that something seemed to be hindering me from reading. Around midday I told myself, I've got my Bible, my sandwiches, and someone is meeting me. As if I needed to convince myself that it was all really happening and I wasn't embarking on a dream journey.

I ate my packed lunch, like Abraham—not knowing whither.[2] Eventually the train arrived at Exeter St. David's station. A few people alighted, and there were others waiting on the platform. I made my way to the exit carrying my suitcase. As I got nearer, I saw a man standing with his arms folded.

That's Bob, said a voice within me.

Bob Love walked toward me, we greeted each other, and confirmed our identities. Taking my case, he led me to his car. I felt strangely tongue-tied as he drove and hoped he wouldn't think me rude as I simply answered his friendly questions but had nothing to say to him.

23 BELMONT ROAD

Soon we arrived at the rear of two large, Georgian-type terraced houses. There was scaffolding against them, and two men were busy working on it. I heard the same voice within me, "This is My house. Everything is done for My glory. You will love everyone here, and they will love you."

I followed Bob in and down into the kitchen, which was in the semi-basement. There I met Norah, his wife, for the first time. Bob left us, and Norah led me up three flights of stairs to the three-bedded room, which had been prepared for me.

"I'll put the kettle on," she said, "and when you're ready, we'll have a cup of tea together." I little knew that this was the beginning of what became a close, lifelong friendship.

The house was simple but homey and welcoming. The dining room, a reclaimed cellar, was off the kitchen. The wooden floor was rough and the walls were bare brick; but to me, feeling secure in believing it was where God had brought me and sensing His presence, it was Heaven on earth! Material things don't compare with the genuine love and welcome I received.

Over the evening meal, I met the other people who lived or stayed in the house. I could feel God's love and was aware that the others had experienced their own encounter with God. This brought a feeling of oneness. One of the men, John Williams, who had been working on the scaffold when I arrived, lived in a flat in the adjacent house number 25 and cared for his invalid wife, Enid, as well as working on the alterations being done to the two houses. He was a fatherly sort of figure and

I felt warmed by his interest in me. To my surprise, he addressed me during the meal, "This is God's house, everything is done for His glory, and everyone will love you here."

"THIS IS GOD'S HOUSE, EVERYTHING IS DONE FOR HIS GLORY, AND EVERYONE WILL LOVE YOU HERE."

I felt I had come home!

Bob, Norah, and the other "brothers and sisters," as we were all called, made me feel special and loved in a wonderful way. I'm sure there were things that weren't perfect, but I wasn't aware of any. Brian, the other man on the scaffold, was not very much younger than me and treated me like a sister. John, the older man, had a married son and daughter. He assured me that he loved Brian and me as much as he did them. I believed him. I felt free and at home but knew these people were enjoying something I had yet to comprehend. John had a very kindly disposition, and I knew that I wanted to talk to him more.

Suddenly, during the meal he said, "When we've finished supper, I'd like us to go up into the living room for a chat." After we had finished eating, we went upstairs where he enquired, "Do you know exactly what the Lord has done for you?" He talked about the accomplishment of Jesus on the cross. When he referred to the Bible, I commented, "I don't know much about the Bible, but I know the stories in there are only stories. They didn't really happen."

He corrected me emphatically, "Every word of the Bible is true!"

We talked for some time. I learned a great deal and was grateful for his interest and faith, which was an inspiration. While I was ill, I had lost interest, confidence, and ability in skills that were easy before, like cooking, dressmaking, and knitting. I believed that I would never be able to do them again. When I mentioned this to John, he told me, "God has taken away your natural abilities. He will give them back to you, but it will be in His strength and with His enabling and for His glory, not your own."

He told me how, when God began to move in his life, he owned a cow. He said he found he could no longer even milk it. He had lost his ability. But when God filled him with His Holy Spirit, he was so full of the love of God that he even went out and kissed the cow! He was also able to milk it again too. John was one of the most gifted men I've known, also a man of great faith and love.

I would often bemoan my state to him, and he would encourage me about the Lord Jesus, "He died for you!" He would say over and over again.

"But..." I would begin.

One day he said, "Jesus took you to the cross when He died, beloved, and you died with Him, but this wretched little girl Jean keeps lifting her head again." I saw it! Keep my head down and my mouth shut was the best thing.

I never knew until thirty-seven years later, when a friend told me, that John had been so perturbed that I had given up my son; yet I had obviously met God, that he prayed and asked God to help him understand. God brought into his mind the story of Solomon and the two women who came to him when one of their babies had died. They argued, and the one whose baby had died said hers was the live one. Solomon asked for a sword and commanded the live baby to be cut in half, at which the real mother said, "Let her have the baby." Solomon's answer was, "Give the child to her; she is the real mother."[3] God used this story to show John my true love for my own son in giving him up.

HEALING EMOTIONAL WOUNDS

No one ever asked or challenged me about my circumstances, which I so appreciated. In the beginning, I wanted to keep a link with Matthew. I had his father's address and would send the odd toy to him. God was beginning to heal my heart. He was enabling me to live without Matthew, but part of me was finding it difficult to let go. I soon realized that before long Matthew would be old enough to wonder where the presents came from. I didn't want to provoke any questions that would cause a problem for him or his father. I had to make a decision again not to send anything else. I never heard from his father, nor expected to, except on one occasion when concerned about something regarding

Matthew, he phoned me. He realized I was not in a position to help and never phoned again.

At first, after I was parted from Matthew I felt a kind of mourning. I didn't want to eat. I even felt I shouldn't smile or laugh. I would try not to enter into any humor at the meal table. It was a form of punishment I was putting myself through. I felt I must carry my grief.

I also was in a tormented state where mixing with others was concerned. I didn't know how to be attentive to others' needs and would pass things at the table when they weren't needed and couldn't relax. Then one morning when I smiled someone commented, happily, that my face had shone. I realized how unnatural and forlorn I must have looked and that this wasn't the way I had to live. From then on I shared mutual enjoyment.

I was still smoking a few cigarettes a day, which Bob and Norah permitted if I kept to my room to smoke them. I came to the end of a packet and decided not to buy any more. Suddenly and unexpectedly, a parcel arrived from someone I had met in hospital. The parcel contained 160 cigarettes! Before I thought much about it I opened a packet. My cigarette lighter was broken and I was using matches. As I took out the last match in the box the Lord said to me, "Don't buy any more matches!" With that I was free. I took all the cigarettes to Bob and asked him to burn them. His face was a picture of delight. He knew I was free. I have never wanted one since.

After the relevant period of time, the divorce my husband had taken against me became absolute. For some reason the papers were delivered by a policeofficer. I felt gripped with finality of it all. Although it was inevitable, I hadn't felt prepared and the clause giving me access to my son, should I want it, really hit me. Knowing the decision I had made, it was like saying goodbye for the second time. The reality that there was no going back was painful. I must have looked in a state of shock as the policeman sent Bob to me. I had to turn my heart toward the Lord. Often a choice is ours but at times it is at our cost. It's on those occasions that we find our Savior's grace. The words of a hymn we sang became very meaningful to me…

> *I worship thee, sweet Will of God*
> *And all thy ways adore,*

And every day I live I long
To love thee more and more.
He always wins who sides with God,
To him no chance is lost;
God's will is sweetest to him when
It triumphs at his cost.
Ill that He blesses is our good;
And unblest good is ill;
And all is right that seems most wrong
If it be His sweet Will"[4]

This comforted me, knowing it was God's will for me to have given up my son. My illness had been blessed as it brought me to Himself; and to others what might have seemed most wrong, was right for me.

We can look back, like Lot's wife, or let God lead us on with Himself. In His faithfulness, He began to strengthen me. There were times when, seeing a mother with her small child, I would have to come to terms with my own loss. Again, the certain knowledge that God knew and cared helped and strengthened me. One day Brian was praying with me, and in his prayer mentioned God having given up His own Son.

THE CERTAIN KNOWLEDGE THAT GOD KNEW
AND CARED HELPED AND STRENGTHENED ME.

This was a great comfort to me.

Many years later, knowing I was distressed about something, Norah wrote to me and said, "Let God minister to you."

We can choose to hang on to our grief almost like a penance at times, as if we ought to feel bad about something. That's what I did at first. But we shut God out of our hearts by doing so. By responding to His love and kindness and allowing Him access to our emotions, He is able to heal and mend our broken hearts. The pain is often in opening up our hearts, it is not He who hurts us. Every mourning has to come to an end.

God wants to heal all our wounds. This was a time of healing for me.

By faith Abraham obeyed when he was called to go out to the place which he would receive as an inheritance. And he went out, not knowing where he was going. By faith he dwelt in the land of promise as in a foreign country, dwelling in tents with Isaac and Jacob the heirs with him of the same promise (Hebrews 11:8-9).

ENDNOTES

1. Joseph Parker, hymn, God Holds the Key.

2. See Hebrews 11:8.

3. See First Kings 3:25-27.

4. Frederick W. Faber, hymn, I worship Thee sweet Will of God.

Chapter Ten

Only He Knows

Faith knows nought of dark tomorrow
For my Savior goes before.[1]

DECEIVED IN EARLY LIFE

During my two-year engagement to Matthew's father, he decided to break it off, largely because of arguments I picked with him where his mother and family were concerned. He said he would not see me for a week while he thought. I found this hard to accept. My colleagues at work were very understanding. One of them, a Catholic, trying to comfort me, wanted to take me to light a candle in a nearby church. This didn't have much meaning for me. She then suggested I go to see a fortune teller with her. This didn't seem wrong or strange to me.

Was I naïve? Maybe. Insecure? Certainly. Blind? Definitely.

I went with Edna one evening after work. The woman she took me to see was in London near where we worked. The little stair-case that led straight off the road was narrow and steep. Edna sat in a waiting room while I was ushered into a dimly lit room. The woman sitting across the table from me, who professed to have these powers, looked pretty ordinary to the innocent eye.

Sitting down, I gave her no details.

"Your birthday is March 24!" she said.

She had my attention.

"March 25." I corrected her.

She looked unperturbed at the correction. She was only a day out.

I wanted this to work. I very much wanted this to work.

"A dark-haired, young man came into the room with you," she announced. My fiancé had dark hair but she didn't mention my broken engagement. I did.

She then said, "I see the initial M." I took this to be Michael, the young man I had met and fallen in love with a few years before and had difficulty forgetting. According to her, I apparently was going to travel. She said, "I see water." None of this meant a thing to me.

She looked at my palm and into her crystal ball, which she uncovered on the table. Foretelling that I would marry the man to whom I had been engaged, she said, "You will have two children." I took all this in hook, line, and sinker! It wasn't difficult to believe as this all fitted in with what I wanted to happen in my life.

During the breakdown I had when Matthew was a baby, I kept remembering the predictions of this fortune teller. Not knowing better, I was convinced everything should happen as she had said. After I was discharged from the first hospital, I saw the Psychiatrist as an outpatient. I mentioned to him that I was considering having another child and asked what he thought.

"Ask me in six months time," he said.

I'm so thankful he said this. It must have been within six months that my marriage ended. It would have been a bigger disaster had I been pregnant as well.

I can see I was trying to will all the fortune teller had said to make it happen.

When I met Mr. North[2] for the first time on arriving in Exeter, I began to explain the inner thoughts, fears, and the sense of a conflicting influence I was experiencing on a day-to-day basis that troubled me. He looked straight at me and asked very directly, "Have you ever been to see a fortune teller?"

When I replied yes, he didn't seem surprised. He then explained to me that there are only two sources of information and power—God or the devil.

THERE ARE ONLY TWO SOURCES OF INFORMATION
AND POWER—GOD OR THE DEVIL.

In going to the fortune teller, I had opened myself to evil spirits that she operated by, and their power was interfering with my life. These spirits had been this woman's source, and I didn't realize I was being affected by demonic forces.

Mr. North, on the other hand, was a man of God and, thankfully, God gave him the discernment and authority to cut me off from this influence. He prayed in the Name of Jesus, binding any spirits and severing ties that bound me to her words.

Jesus set me free and the power was broken. This brought release in many areas of my life.

How unwittingly we can fall foul of the devil who works in darkness. He takes advantage of those who, through ignorance, wander into his territory, usually tempted by inquisitiveness or drawn by a strange fancy for the unknown. His bait takes many forms; and even things that appear innocent, like horoscopes, bring darkness and have hooks in their tails.

We must renounce all dealings with the occult. The Bible warns us these practices are wrong. God hates them. Jesus is the only true Source of all light. If we abide in His light we remain free from the powers of darkness. The only place of safety is in placing our future into His hands. Only He knows our destiny.

Whereas the devil tried to destroy me, God is greater and had a future for me.

Do not turn to mediums or seek out spiritists, for you will be defiled by them. I am the Lord your God (Leviticus 19:31).

I will set my face against anyone who turns to mediums and spiritists to prostitute themselves by following them, and I will cut them off from their people (Leviticus 20:6).

Let no one be found among you who sacrifices their son or daughter in the fire, who practices divination or sorcery, interprets omens, engages in witchcraft, or casts spells, or who is a medium or spiritist or who consults the dead. Anyone who does these things is detestable to the Lord; because of these same detestable practices the Lord your God will drive out those nations before you (Deuteronomy 18:10-12).

ENDNOTES

1. F. Bottome, hymn, Full Salvation!

2. Please visit Mr. North website to read about his teachings: www.biblebase.com

Chapter Eleven

Life at 23 Belmont Road

He [God] *sets the solitary in families.*[1]

A HOME

Someone described me as a daughter of the house. I certainly loved living in number 23 Belmont Road. It was to me a privilege and responsibility. I felt the security of feeling wanted and loved but also a sure sense of being in God's will. There was very much a sense of the now. The Lord had taken and forgiven the past. He was healing my heart and memory, and showing me how His hand had been on my life from an early age. The future I left with Him, as He had spoken to me that "this home is for life." Whatever life meant!

People came and went for various reasons, staying while in the area, or for holidays. Often people would stay because they needed help and ministry. The fact that Mr. North lived next door brought many who needed to speak to him over a period of time. Having been in great need myself, and still feeling it in some areas, gave me an understanding where some were concerned, which God in His grace used and blessed.

BOB AND NORAH TRUSTED GOD FOR EVERYTHING.

Conferences were held from time to time in the Fellowship. Mr. North's teaching and preaching meant the house would be full of people staying over. They came for ministry that many wouldn't have the chance to hear otherwise. This resulted in the home being very busy, with many beds to make and rooms to be prepared. There was also a lot of food preparation and cooking to be done. Money wasn't plentiful, and Bob and Norah trusted God for everything. These were the days before freezers. I remember the first one given was an old commercial ice cream chest freezer. John Williams didn't approve as he said the Lord told us to take no thought what we should eat. The value of having one, practically and financially, won the day! Norah and I learned how to prepare and blanch vegetables when in season, baking in advance, and storing surplus cooked food for a later occasion. The ice cream freezer was later replaced with a more sophisticated domestic model.

Number 23 was on five floors. The kitchen, dining room, and laundry were in the reclaimed semi-basement. On the ground floor was the meeting room, which was L-shaped, being two large rooms knocked into one. Along the wall at the front were French windows, which at one time would have opened onto a covered veranda. Another veranda ran across the back linking the two houses. From the hall, the staircase leading to all the floors had a lovely polished banister. The first floor comprised of three rooms. The large lounge had big windows, a high ceiling, and marble fireplace. As there was no central heating then, an oil stove sat in the fireplace. Because of my happy state of peace and well-being in those days, the smell of an oil fire is still pleasant to me.

Bob's study was next to the lounge at the front of the house; and he could be found sitting at his huge desk, welcoming all, especially visitors. Bob would sacrifice his study on occasions, and it became the overflow bedroom. Bob and Norah's own bedroom was also on this floor, and a small toilet. On the next floor there were bathrooms and bedrooms, one of which was the original one I had and shared with whoever else was staying. Bob said I should have my own room, and I was given a little single room in the corner at the front, which until then had been called "The prophet's chamber," named after the room the widow prepared for Elisha.[2] This remained my room until circumstances changed.

At the top of the house were attic rooms.

Bob was a fatherly figure. He had been a captain in the army and only on one occasion did he enthral us, one evening in the lounge, when he told us the story of how he was injured and captured. He remained a prisoner of war. He and Norah were married during the war in India where Norah had been born and brought up. Knowing he was to be sent abroad, they brought their wedding date forward. Married just ten days, Bob was sent overseas. They never saw each other again until Bob's repatriation two years before the war ended. Bob became a bank manager overseas. They lived abroad as ex pats, with the privilege and lifestyle that went with the job.

Norah, brought up with a similar lifestyle, was used to having servants and cooks. Not being an idle woman, she learned and taught feminine skills such as ballet and flower arranging. She was very gifted at being a hostess and entertaining and incorporated these skills as she served the Lord in the house.

Bob had a big heart and a great gift for making people feel special. In his desk was a large book marked Member's Roll in which he entered the names and addresses of people to whom he talked in the study. On the wall of his study was a map of the British Isles. In these days God was moving, and Fellowships were springing up all over the country. Bob kept a box of colored drawing pins. As he heard of groups of people meeting together, he would put one of the drawing pins in the appropriate place on the map. These multiplied "like mushrooms" as someone had prophesied that the fellowships would. Bob would often refer to the map when a visitor mentioned a place where they or someone else lived who had no Fellowship. He would get out the Member's Roll book and linked people together continually, often using the colored drawing pins.

Mr. North would visit these young groups who wanted teaching on Church life, and he would minister from a scriptural base.

VALUABLE LESSONS

I'm grateful for the lessons I learned in just passing on an address to someone alone who didn't know there were fellow believers near them. I learned the discipline of making visitors welcome on Bob and Norah's behalf. Often there were too many for them to greet at one time. I would have to give an answer if, selfishly, I had just spent time with a friend after a meeting, leaving a visitor feeling unwelcome. This is vital for church growth and is important in developing a more outgoing personality, doing away with self-preservation in hiding behind cups of tea. My own upbringing was far removed from this lifestyle, and I am glad the Lord educated me this way.

MY FIRST REACTION WAS TO PANIC, BUT I REMEMBERED
MY PRAYER AND LOOKED TO THE LORD FOR HELP.

When I first went to Belmont Road, I found mixing impossible. The constant flow of visitors was painful for me. After an initial introduction, I would head for the door and escape to my room. On one such occasion, I sat on my bed, having left the visitors talking with Bob and Norah.

The Lord spoke to me, "Now what?"

I repeated to Him, "Now what?"

I could hear the laughter coming from everyone downstairs.

Who was the loser? Me!

I prayed that the next time visitors came the Lord would help me not to run away. Soon afterward I saw a group of people walking up the path to the back door. My first reaction was to panic, but I remembered my prayer and looked to the Lord for help. The visitors came in and I helped Norah serve tea and coffee. Then Norah offered to show them around. At which point one young woman announced, "I'll just stay here with Jean." When everyone had gone she confessed to me that she had been terrified of coming into the house until she had seen me in the kitchen, through the window. She said, "For some reason I felt I would be safe with you!"

GOD NOT ONLY HAS A SENSE OF HUMOR BUT CERTAINLY HAS
ORDINARY METHODS OF SETTING US FREE FROM OURSELVES AT TIMES.

God not only has a sense of humor but certainly has ordinary methods of setting us free from ourselves at times. I found this was true for me. I never ran again and learned that the person you fear often feels worse than you do. If we can forget about ourselves and move out to others, we often free ourselves. This no longer presented a problem for me.

Another lesson learned was from Mr. North's daughter, Marian. In the early days, I was frequently in tears. Memories and feelings that were still difficult to come to terms with gave me a sense of inadequacy. I felt I needed to be understood because of it.

One day Marian, a very loving person, simply said to me, "If you make your need your security it's sin!" I realized the truth of this and that is what I was, in fact, doing. I had to discipline myself where this was concerned. The Scripture says, "Faithful are the wounds of a friend."[3] How faithful are those who care enough to speak words of life.

Many years later I was spending time with Andy and his wife, Margie, whom I had met in the beginning. Margie said, "You have to turn your back on your need!" I saw how necessary it is to do this.

At first I thought I could never be like the Christians who surrounded me. It was Brian who spoke in a very straight but truthful way this time asking me, "What makes you think you are so special that God can't do it for you?" I knew Brian loved me and that God loved me. It was unbelief on my part to think these thoughts. Although I couldn't change myself, God could. I had to take my eyes off myself and on to Him and believe Him to do the work in me.

Norah was a very positive person, whereas my own mother had been extremely negative. I had taken on her mental attitude. I soon realized there was a different way of reacting to situations and viewing things. As much as possible I would follow Norah's example.

She also taught me to do everything as unto the Lord, not to please men. If what we do is for Him, we don't get hurt when someone doesn't appreciate or approve of what we do. It is for Him. She also instilled into me that it is worse to take offence than to give it!

It was also from Norah that I learned how important it is to develop a real and personal relationship with Jesus.

LIVING TOGETHER

When I first arrived in the house, the laundry room didn't exist, all the ironing was done in the only private room that Bob and Norah had, their bedroom. One of their daughters found it hard when visiting her parents as it was difficult to be alone with them. That didn't hinder the friendship I enjoyed with Wendy who would often call me to join them on the occasions when I tried to make myself scarce. She actually asked me to go and live with her and her family when they lived in Worcester. But I didn't feel this was God's call.

Soon after I came to Belmont Road another woman came to stay. Her name was Dot. She too was from London. She also had a difficult time in life and had come to seek the Lord. We became friends although living very differently in the house. Mr. North's spoken ministry was being recorded onto the old type of reel tape by Peter Palmer, a brother who lived in number 21, until Dot proved her skills in the area of audio recording. Pete would let the tape recorder run for the whole course of the meeting. Dot occupied one of the attic rooms, and before long started to edit and re-record tapes in her own bedroom. Bob also appreciated her secretarial skills. In later years she began the work of putting Mr. North's tapes into print by sitting with a tape recorder and typing directly from the tapes. This work was taken over by Pat, a sister who had been blessed while staying in Belmont Road. She lived in Dorset as a midwife and began to print the manuscripts on a Bandar machine. Mr. North by this time was writing books which later, along with these, were put into the book form many of us know. Thanks to modern technology these are now available for reading on a Website as well.

IF WE WERE IN ANY WAY CONCERNED ABOUT ANYTHING
WE WERE PREPARING, WE WOULD PRAY.

The days in Exeter were simple. It was the practice for everyone to stay for lunch after church on Sunday. As the Fellowship grew, so did the size of saucepans we used each week for meals. There wasn't any awareness of a shelf life or of having to consume things by a use-by date then, and no one ever got sick or suffered any ill effects. Usually if we were in any way concerned about anything we were preparing, we would pray—one of the things Norah taught me to do. I'd like to testify that this meant where quantity was a concern as well. I've known us to prepare a meal, in good faith, believing we had made enough, only to find we had more visitors than we had anticipated. It was a matter of just not hesitating while serving, but trusting and keeping on spooning! A knowing look at each other and an upward glance often confirmed that the amount of food on everyone's plate was obviously more than we had cooked. Well, if the Lord could do it for 5,000, He could do it for 50!

During those years, lifelong friendships were made. The one uniting factor was the love of Jesus in everyone's heart.

There were difficulties at times. No people, however saintly, can live together without times of testing, anything else would be unreal. Some saw those living in the house as doormats and to be taken for granted. One sister, who came to a deeper relationship with the Lord later herself, confessed this to me saying, "I thought I could do anything to you!"

At such times it made the teaching of the cross invaluable. Our self-life always feels it has a right. Jesus teaches that we have no rights to ourselves. That isn't easy. In our own strength we can't give up our rights to ourselves; but yielding to His cross, He makes a way. One of the young women we knew once wrote a hymn that said, "Jesus, Thy cross is sweet to me."[4]

It was a privilege to be with people whose lives were evidences of this. I used to say we had the loveliest people in the world cross our threshold. Many men of God visited, both to preach or just as friends of Bob and Norah.

I remember sitting in the garden peeling a large pot of potatoes when Harry Greenwood came and sat on the bench beside me and talked with me. Harry was a renowned figure in Christian circles, known for his ministry, mainly in preaching. Name-dropping doesn't come into an encounter with such a godly man who had come to visit Bob and Norah because he had heard of Wendy's death. Harry had stayed with the family in the days when he owned nothing, appreciating their friendship just for themselves. It is good to know from what small beginnings some men of faith have grown. It also explains much.

One thing I remember Harry said, when speaking about the Lord prospering a person, "If people can't see Jesus because of your car, get rid of it!" He was also known to be a very loving man.

CHERISHED FRIENDS

Edgar Parkyns, a missionary who was dear to many in person and by his ministry, also owned a house in Belmont Road. When home from abroad, Africa or later on America, he would turn up unannounced. It would cheer the heart to suddenly hear his voice as he took part from the back of the meeting room. Much later when I lived alone, he would include me in his visits. The first time he came to seek me out and I answered the door, leaning on the roof of a parked car he said, "I've forgotten my excuse. Oh yes, I'm selling matches!"

Though a broken, sensitive man, Edgar had a rare sense of humor. He used this on one occasion when he asked me to look at a sewing machine he had bought for his daughter. After I had proved my ability to use the machine, he then asked if I would be able to convert a jacket pocket in a certain way making it more secure for travelling. Having assured him I could, he produced the jacket along with a matching reel of thread, twinkling with an impish grin. I had walked straight into his plan. I loved Edgar, and I knew he did me. I enjoyed a wonderful understanding with him. Edgar went to be with the Lord in 1987.

There were two elderly ladies with whom I became close. Jo had never married; she lived alone in a large house, which she turned into rented flats. She lived in the middle flat. She explained she didn't want the responsibility of the garden and the stairs gave her exercise! I loved "Old Jo," as she was called, and she me. Jo considered herself a founding member of the Fellowship, as she had been among those who met with Bob and Norah from the beginning. Yet she still remained a British Israelite,[5] strangely enough. She looked on Bob like a son and they shared a love for each other.

THE EXAMPLE AND EXPRESSION OF THE FATHER HEART
OF GOD GAVE ME A VALUABLE FOUNDATION.

Marie lived in a little village outside Exeter and caught a bus in each week. She lived alone, beside her daughter and family. Marie had been widowed during the war, bringing up four children with devotion, love, and faith. I learned a lot from her life. I went to her funeral at the end of 2004, having seen her just a few months before in a nursing home in Exeter. She died at 104 years of age! Meetings are, at the time of writing, still being held in the nursing home as a result of Marie's life, witness, and request.

What inspiration and example, just a few of many!

Little did Bob and Norah know when they said the home was there for as long as I liked, that I'd be there for almost ten years! And I didn't realize either that things weren't always to continue as they were. The example and expression of the Father heart of God I had been shown over these years gave a foundation that would prove to be of such value to me for the future.

I didn't know what lay ahead.

So Jesus answered and said, "Assuredly, I say to you, there is no one who has left house or brothers or sisters or father or mother or wife or children or lands, for My sake and the gospel's, who shall not receive a hundredfold now in this time—houses and brothers and sisters and mothers and children and lands, with persecutions—and in the age to come, eternal life" (Mark 10:29).

ENDNOTES

1. See Psalm 68:6.

2. See Second Kings 4:10.

3. See Proverbs 27:6.

4. Carole German.

5. A British Israelite is one who believes that the British originate from the twelve lost tribes of Israel.

Heaven's Door

I came to you a stranger
I knocked upon heaven's door.
No other door was there for me,
Nowhere the misery of heart to pour.

I knocked, I couldn't look,
Dare hoping you'd give me voice.
It seemed an age for to be heard.
Tho' patient in this choice

I little knew before I knocked
You'd seen me as I made my way
And had prepared for me a room,
Knowing that you'd bid to stay.

Before I e'en did state my case
I looked and saw within your eyes
A look that said you knew it all
I could say nought that would surprise.

While I withstood at distance
Your love enveloped me
It drew me nearer, nearer
Till all I knew was Thee.

The pain had gone tho' scars remained.
Now even these have faded.
The balm of Thy forgiving love
Left the cause of fear unaided.

Now in the light of battle won
My future is secure.
I've time to spend in seeking
Other souls to procure.

My heart is free forever,
And only feels Thy love.
But while I wait, I wonder
Will it burst with joy above?

Chapter Twelve

Not as I Will, Nevertheless...[1]

No matter if the way be sometimes dark,
No matter though the cost be oft-times great,
He knoweth how I best shall reach the mark,
The way that leads to Him must needs be straight.[2]

This chapter has caused me much heart searching and has been extremely difficult to write. I would that it didn't need to be included. It is now over 30 years since what I am about to relate took place, but the course of my life was changed for ever, therefore it is pivotal in my story. The cause of it may not be understood but its effect and outcome cannot be underestimated.

THE SUDDEN LOSS OF BOB

We little knew how suddenly everything would change.

Bob lived life to the full, but his days were numbered, he wasn't a fit man. Whether it was the years of being a prisoner of war or a result of the operation after being injured and captured I'm not sure, but his heart was not strong. Norah secretly worried about him. He didn't spare himself. There were able brothers who had arrived over the years to shoulder some of the responsibilities but Bob's big heart kept him committed to his shepherd's role.

After one health scare, his friend Jack Kelly, a doctor who led a Fellowship in Scotland, advised him to restrict his movements by staying on the first floor. There he had all the facilities he needed, including his study. He was to reduce his weight too. Bob submitted to all of this, remaining confined to these quarters for three months. At the end of this period he set about life with a fresh zeal. On the Sunday afternoon he even played a little game of football with his grandsons in the garden. Looking on, one felt that he just wanted to live.

It had been arranged the following day that a couple of brothers staying in the house would go fishing early in the morning. Coming down into the kitchen first thing, one of them found Bob. The Lord had taken him to be with Himself. In 1975 Bob died.

NORAH'S REACTION

Although an early riser, Norah was still asleep. Knocking on her bedroom door, they woke her and broke the news that Bob had gone.

Later she shared with me her immediate response which had a profound effect on me.

She simply said, "Lord, I'm expecting You to take me into a deeper relationship with Yourself."

Three weeks later, in a meeting, she testified that this is what God had done for her. She missed Bob, yet grief is a necessary part of healing where loss has left a painful gap. Years later she wrote to me that God had healed her heart, but that didn't alter the reality that her status had changed for the rest of her life, and a human relationship she had enjoyed was over.

There were many changes ahead, and I confess I was unprepared for some. I didn't realize how they would affect my own life. Norah was bereaved of a beloved husband. I was later to know a grief and bereavement of a different kind.

UNEXPECTED CHANGE

Reflecting over the next period is painful and difficult. But my memory has strangely been refreshed, as I find myself 35 years on, staying in the Fellowship house in Reading. The kitchen is a reminder because the layout and geography is virtually identical to the kitchen I referred to in Belmont Road, Exeter.

When a father dies, the children have to learn to grow up. God had brought me a long way. Fears, inhibitions, and even imaginations rooted in past experiences take time to be broken. With no immediate family, being single again had been made easier for me by the love, support, and security I found in responsible brothers God placed in the church. I saw these in place of a husband. As God was healing my heart and setting me free spiritually, there would be times I would seek help and prayer from these men. I saw them as God's provision. Equally, the godly women were an inspiration and similar help at times, and I sought to follow their example. Out east, as we say, a young ox would be yoked to an older ox to teach it to walk a straight path. God gave me many older oxen during those years.

FEARS, INHIBITIONS, AND EVEN IMAGINATIONS ROOTED
IN PAST EXPERIENCES TAKE TIME TO BE BROKEN.

Life in the house resumed normality after Bob's death. Norah showed a wonderful spirit. She continued to work and serve in number 23, running the domestic side of things, but she moved into the flat in number 25 while the couple who were there moved over to run number 23. This couple, with two small children, had come to stay some time earlier while Bob and Norah were away. After Bob and Norah returned they stayed on as part of the family in the house. They had fitted into the house and we all enjoyed easy relationships. He was gifted and able with a strong personality but now he assumed a leadership role.

The old order gives place to the new. In this new situation I found a change of a different kind and a different sort of headship.

I soon discovered I was under a new Pharaoh.

Naively perhaps and, I confess, brushing aside doubt, I approached this brother who was now seen to replace Bob in the home. Not realizing I was making myself vulnerable, I shared a need of my heart with him. Until then, he had given every indication that I was as valued and an equal, where respect was concerned, as the others were. At first I interpreted the lack of response as a sign of not wanting to speak hastily because he wanted to think before giving me any counsel or prayer. I was unsuspecting and didn't anticipate it was the beginning of a distancing, which eventually led to an estrangement.

Some weeks later I was summoned to the study and told that I needed a new move of God in my life; that I should move out of the house and find a job and flat. This was foreign to what I had heard from any brother previously. I couldn't really take it in. Perhaps I didn't want to. I certainly didn't feel prepared or know what God wanted me to do.

PRESSURE

I found myself under instruction for the first time. Situations were put to me that I was informed were considered to be God's will for me. Some of these entailed moving, but I declined when it came to moving to another part of the country. This was met with disapproval. I no longer felt free.

When I was told there was a need in the Birmingham Fellowship house and this was God's will for me, I felt it would be better to move. I knew the couple who led it and thought I would accept and trust the Lord and got as far as obtaining a cardboard box to start packing my belongings. When I announced that I was prepared to go, it was met with great pleasure.

A few days later I was summoned and displeasure shown as I was told the position had been filled, and I was no longer needed.

God had firmly closed the door!

After that the pressure seemed relentless. My duties were changed in the house, and I was forbidden to help Norah any longer in the kitchen. Instead, I was to take on the cleaning in number 25 as well as number 23. I was also to help two families with large houses in Exeter!

Next door in number 21, Tony and Sheila's house, there was a small attic room that became vacant. This was put to me as my answer to moving out. I was, by this time, already helping Sheila with the cleaning of her house. Imagining myself cooped up alone in a small room seemed like a remedy for disaster; it would stifle all the Lord had been doing in me. I declined.

The pressure I found myself under developed into personal, verbal attacks.

No one had ever taken it on themselves to instruct me as to what God's will for my life was on a day-to-day basis. Nor had anyone before insisted, in such a manner, that I obey what tasks and duties they found for me to do.

On one occasion he asked me if I had told anyone how he was speaking to me.

I did not know what to say and there was no other elder in the church at that time. I felt alone in my plight. The only person I spoke to about it was Norah, who would almost always have the mind of the Spirit. She was at a loss to know what to say to me. I felt the safest way was silence.

COUSIN MIKE

On one of my cousin Mike's visits, I was dismayed and humiliated when I was asked, in front of a table full of people if I had found a flat and a job yet! Dumbfounded, I simply said no. I was surprised that Mike never questioned me about this afterward.

I hadn't known that, to strengthen his position, this brother had taken Mike into his confidence and persuaded him that the course of action he was taking was right. Whatever he had said to Mike seemed to change the way he viewed me and his manner became different. Our relationship was permanently damaged. This, in turn, reflected in his mother's attitude toward me when, years later, she disowned me in her will.

IT IS GOOD TO KNOW GOD AND REST IN THE KNOWLEDGE
THAT HE IS A GOD OF TRUTH AND JUSTICE.

At such times it is good to know God and rest in the knowledge that He is a God of truth and justice. He knows everything.

The confusion and insecurity that all this brought about made it difficult to publicly maintain an outward appearance that all was well. Deep within I couldn't accept what was happening as it contradicted all I had known and enjoyed, not only within the church, but of God's character. I suppose I began to serve two masters. What I'm sure appeared disobedience to one, often proved to be confirmed right by the other I knew within my heart. It was not the shock of being told to leave the house but the shaking of my whole foundation in knowing God's voice and will that took place. Perhaps had it come with the same reassuring tone familiar to me, I wouldn't have felt so unsure. I was being made to feel unwanted, especially when I was told, "I don't have to inherit you!" This I took to refer to the fact I had been taken in by Bob.

The situation continued for many months. Accusations were made against me, and I knew I couldn't do a thing that would be considered right or acceptable. I was also becoming afraid of being alone with this man. On such occasions, the opportunity was always abused by further innuendoes and criticism.

When he started making sinister statements like, "You are going insane." And "You are going to have a breakdown." I knew not to heed these, and rejected them.

I felt I could go on no longer and not knowing what to do I asked Norah, as I often did, to pray with me. I felt quite desperate as we knelt together.

"Please Lord, remove me from this situation or take my life."

Norah stopped me, "I can't agree to a prayer like that," she said.

She told me later it was then she realized how desperate I was becoming and she was very concerned for me. Neither of us had spoken to anyone else about this.

But God had heard.

MISS MORTIMER

At the back of number 23, facing the parking space , there was a very large Victorian house. A Christian family, the Mortimers, had lived there for a couple of generations. As they had become old, one by one they all died apart from one last remaining member of the family. She had no one to care for her except a nephew who visited her each Saturday. About a week after Norah and I prayed, Miss

Mortimer approached the brother who was running number 23 and asked if there was anyone who could go and live with her as a companion. This was put to me again as God's will for me.

The role of companion included shopping and cooking for Miss Mortimer; in exchange, I would be given a lounge and bedroom, board free. Feeling able to meet the criteria and seeing this as an escape, I accepted and moved in.

HALFORD HOUSE

In Halford House, Miss Mortimer's home, I was given two large rooms, furnished with what were probably valuable antiques, in exchange for my role as companion/shopper/cook. Miss Mortimer wasn't difficult to cook for. She was disciplined and frugal despite the fact she was obviously very wealthy. There was also a gardener and cleaner who kept everything in order.

It was like stepping back in time. The house would have been beautiful in its day. Everything was in its original state. The furniture in the huge reception rooms on the ground floor was Victorian. Two of these rooms, with high ceilings and large fireplaces with over-mantles, were joined by folding doors, creating one enormous room.

On the top floor, the bedroom furniture in each room was of matching wood. An old fashioned wash-hand stand stood in each of these rooms. Miss Mortimer herself still used one. There was no hot running water or heating in the house.

Our relationship was a strange one.

The fact that at first Miss Mortimer wanted me in by 10 at night and refused to give me a key didn't make life easy. I decided to submit for a month, after which it got a bit easier when she gave me a key. I reported every Saturday to her nephew when he visited. He seemed to enjoy the coffee and chat more than wanting to ask questions about life in his aunt's house.

My heart had to gradually let
go of all that I held dear.

I took in sewing for pocket money and was free to visit friends and baby-sit for those with small children. I was still cleaning three large houses, but the duties in 23 and 25 had been taken over by my replacement. Strangely I was expected to carry on doing all the laundry. This I did until I found it practically impossible. Watching it pour with rain on three clothes lines of washing while fulfilling my commitment across the street made this clear.

My heart had to gradually let go of all that I held dear. It was like saying goodbye to a life. A life I loved for almost ten years in Belmont Road. The choice was not mine.

THE CHAPEL

The Fellowship had grown and, as a church, we were seeking the Lord about purchasing or renting a larger building somewhere. The building that is to this day called the "Old Chapel" was found. It was an old church building that was being used as a warehouse and was up for sale. The question of buying it was put to us as a church. The chapel was soon bought for an amazingly modest figure. The enormous task of renovating it and rebuilding the interior for the needs and use of the Fellowship appeared daunting, but everyone rolled up their sleeves and helped. There were a few full-time brothers and unbelievably the building was ready within the year.

The chapel stood on a corner in a prominent position at the far side of the city. I still wanted to be involved in what God was doing in the Fellowship, and I would join those working on the building. To do this and to attend meetings, when they started being held there, meant a walk of at least 30 minutes for me from one end of the city to the other.

One day a week was set aside for prayer, starting with a meeting at 6:30 A.M. This meant a very early start. Being responsible for meals where I lived and not being a driver, I could not attend the meetings held at midday. The evening meetings would start with prayer at 6 P.M. and finish, at times, around 11 PM. I would then have to walk home alone through the city with the cinemas emptying and passing pubs, which I often found terrifying.

THE VASE

Soon after I had moved out of the house, I was child minding for Tony and Sheila, the couple who lived next door in number 21. As I sat quietly alone with two small children, the back door opened and in walked the person I've mentioned, who by then I was trying to avoid. He began another verbal dressing down. I found this particularly distressing, especially as it was in front of these children. He asked me to come to his study next door after Tony and Sheila came home. He wanted to speak to me, saying he had a gift for me. I no longer felt I had to submit to him and said no.

This made him angry and he replied, "You won't even receive a gift from others, like Norah?"

When I heard it was a gift from others I relented and said I would come. It was quite late at night when I went into the house. He gave me a gift-wrapped package. I took it. There was a brief conversation, which I am not able to remember, as I just wanted to leave.

Back in Halford house I opened the package and inside was a beautiful green Wedgwood vase. I put it on the mantle of the bedroom.

When I next saw Norah, I mentioned the vase to thank her. She said she knew nothing about it and neither did anyone else in the house. I took the vase from the mantle-piece, put it back into the box and threw it into the bottom of the wardrobe. I had been tricked.

DIFFICULT DECISION

Apart from the Lord Himself, the church had been my life. The situation now had become too much for me, and I felt I could not go on the way things were. I had to make a decision. I would have to stop attending the meetings in the chapel. It isn't profitable for me to go into all the issues that led to me making this decision. Some circumstances seem unavoidable, and it is at these times it can be difficult to see the hand of God. Sometimes God will take us through extreme situations, never letting go of us, although remaining concealed. With hindsight, I see this was what was happening for me.

Of course, before long, questions were being asked. The children, I was told, asked why Auntie Jean wasn't at the meetings. This proved a problem, not just for me. Going through difficulty is one thing; becoming one to people you love is another. I couldn't see what I could do.

Silence was, for me, the way of safety. But this can also be the way of misunderstanding.

By this time I was unable to function in the way I had previously. My relationship with the brother who had brought about my situation had completely broken down and I would avoid contact with him. When things reached this point, he attempted to offer friendship. He wrote a letter, telling me he "discerned fear" and invited me for coffee with his wife. I felt unable to respond. It seemed casual and incongruous to me, and I held no hope it would alter anything.

I wrote back, declined and took the opportunity to say how I felt.

THE ARRANGED MEETING

The next thing I knew a meeting was arranged by this man. Two other brothers for whom I had a great respect were also present. This was to fulfil the Scripture in Matthew's Gospel that says if someone will not hear you, take one or two more. The fact I didn't want to meet him for coffee must have been seen in this light. We met in one of these brother's homes.

At this meeting I had an unreal feeling about what was taking place and was numb in my pain and fear. He opened the meeting referring to Scriptures then made an attempt at an apology for the situation that had arisen between us. However, because he made an untrue statement which made me feel disadvantaged, hope left me. I am unable to recall what it was he said, but his apology didn't appear genuine to me. I felt under pressure to respond and tried to give an explanation of how I felt.

This was met with, "I can't hear repentance," from him.

Raymond, the brother whose house we were in, said, "That's not what we're here for."

He gently said to me, "Remember Jean, the Lord is coming back."

I warmed to this, but there was nothing I could wring out of my heart toward the brother concerned; it just seemed a procedure that had to be gone through.

This meeting achieved nothing.

THE CHURCH MEETING

Again, following through what Matthew's Gospel says, a church meeting was then called. I was expected to attend. Not knowing what would happen and feeling quite unable to present my case in front of the whole church, I made no attempt to go. I had no desire to do so in any case deciding that whatever would be said would have to be said in my absence.

On the evening of the meeting, I watched from a window in the house where I lived. As the cars left for the meeting I felt as if they were going to my funeral! I sat in a dazed turmoil for the whole of the evening and again watched as they all returned.

I had no idea of the outcome. I was alone in my agony.

THE FINAL BLOW

A few days later, a letter dropped onto the front door mat. The letter accused me of "railing" against this brother. I knew I was not guilty of this but didn't see what I could do about it. I was informed of the conclusion of the meeting. I felt distressed, but I did not realize it was actually a letter of excommunication. I was not only devastated, having been forced to leave the fulfilling life I had loved but, finding myself in the role of the offender, brought a feeling of guilt and disgrace.

"LORD, I DON'T RECEIVE THIS FROM YOU!"

I remember spreading the letter out on the kitchen table and simply saying to the Lord, "I don't receive this from You!" This brought some kind of peace. Much later, when I met Mr. North and told him this, he said, "Good."

After that I tried to live each day as it came. I continued to see my friends and only one or two referred to the meeting and told me some things that had been said; most just treated me as they normally did, almost as though nothing had happened.

Contemplating the future, or even my present situation, seemed beyond me.

MISS MORTIMER'S FAREWELL

One evening, not long afterward, a friend who was a nurse was visiting me. It was God's hand of care, as we heard a noise and ran to see what had happened. Miss Mortimer had fallen down the steps that led from the kitchen to the cellar below onto a stone floor. Although apparently unhurt, Miss Mortimer had come to the beginning of her last days in the house that she had hoped to die in.

She never really recovered from her fall. She had private nursing for a while in her home, then the family arranged for her to go into hospital and from there she was taken into a nursing home. Her nephew told me the family had agreed I was to have free run of the house until I decided what I wanted to do. I was grateful for this as it gave me a little respite and took the pressure off me having to make a decision for the time being.

Soon a new chapter was to open in my life but things were never to be the same for me.

> *For it is not an enemy who reproaches me; then I could bear it. Nor is it one who hates me who has exalted himself against me; Then I could hide from him. But it was you, a man my equal, my companion and my acquaintance. We took sweet counsel together, and walked to the house of God in the throng* (Psalm 55:12-14).

ENDNOTES

1. See Matthew 26:39.

2. Frederick Brook, hymn, My Goal Is God Himself.

Chapter Thirteen

Honor Thy Father and Mother

If of parents I came
Who honoured Thy name,
'Twas thy wisdom appointed it so.
—John Wesley

Snow fell incessantly during the Saturday night before the New Year of 1979. Exeter, where the winters were normally mild, became virtually cut off. In some places the snow drifts reached the eaves of houses!

I planned to visit my parents in London as I usually did for New Year, having spent Christmas in Devon. I recall walking down the high street on Sunday morning; the pavements piled high with snow where the snow ploughs had deposited it. I had to walk in the road where there were skiers skiing! I intended to travel on Monday, but the radio warned that no one should attempt to leave Exeter.

I abandoned the idea.

On arriving at church, I found a young couple from London. Phil came to the Fellowship while at Exeter University. I knew him well and had attended their wedding a few years previously. They were due to return to London the following day, Monday.

"I'm going to London tomorrow, no matter what!" Phil announced.

"If you're going, I'm going with you." I told him.

The next morning, despite the warnings, we slid our way out of Exeter and made our journey through the winter landscape. It was planned that I would be dropped at a certain railway station where I could pick up a train to Welling where my parents lived.

I don't recall the station where I was dropped, but I waved as the car pulled away and turned the corner; my suitcase in my hand, I walked toward the station. The sign that greeted me said, "Trains cancelled or delayed due to weather conditions."

Strangely unperturbed, I walked to the ticket office. Although the station seemed deserted, I was able to buy a ticket. Alone on that cold platform I never entertained the thought that I could be marooned at this unfamiliar station, and I can't remember how long I waited. But, despite the signs to the contrary, a train came along.

I HARDLY REALIZED WHAT A MIRACLE THE JOURNEY WAS.

I hardly realized what a miracle the journey was. I must have made a phone call to let my parents know I was on my way as when I arrived at Welling station, Dad was there to meet me. I was so glad to see him. The heavy snow was nationwide, and the scenery had been a winter one all the way to London—the snow deep there.

Safe at my parent's home, I slept in the small bedroom of their two bedroom house. As I was trying to get to sleep that night, I could hear an unfamiliar dripping sound. I switched on the light, opened the airing cupboard to see if there might be something wrong with the boiler, but could find no explanation. The dripping sounded so close I decided to call Dad.

Dad could hear it too and came to investigate.

The only place we hadn't looked was in the loft. With the aid of a pair of steps Dad climbed up peered into the loft with a torch. When he re-emerged his face was grim.

"There's water dripping down the inside of the roof," he reported, "all around it."

The only thing we could do at that hour was to place bowls, buckets, and receptacles to catch the water. Dad had just retired that year; he was not a practical person, and I could see how worried he was the following day. He didn't know what to do.

I remember thinking that if it had been Exeter, I would have known whom I could call upon, but this was London. Then I remembered the Fellowship in Eltham I visited when staying with my parents. I felt confident I could call them, "After all," I told myself, "we are all one Body."

The man I knew and hoped would be there was Dave, who was not only extremely practical and a good joiner, but had a heart big enough to make everyone feel special. I told him about the water dripping through the roof. Dave spoke in a comforting, matter-of-fact way and said, "Tell your dad not to worry. The snow this year is very fine and has drifted under the slates in roofs where it melts and drips. There is nothing wrong with his roof."

We said goodbye and I thanked him.

Dad seemed comforted by this news and cheered up a little.

After lunch, the door bell rang. Opening the door, to my surprise, there stood Dave with a pair of overalls under his arm. He explained to me that God told him to come. Terry, the pastor of the Fellowship happened to be visiting someone near my parents that afternoon and had dropped him off. He would pick him up later.

Dad and Dave climbed up into the loft.

Dave scraped snow from behind the lining of the roof that would have melted. They handed five buckets of snow to me one at a time to be emptied!

When Dave was satisfied that the snow was cleared, he and Dad reappeared. Mum made tea, and Dave washed simply at the kitchen sink. Over a cup of tea we chatted, Dad obviously warm in his gratitude toward Dave. No sooner was the tea finished than Terry rang the doorbell to collect Dave.

IT WAS LIKE A VISITATION FROM HEAVEN.

Dave was gone.

It was like a visitation from Heaven.

"Where is he from?"

"How did you know him?"

"I didn't give him anything!" Dad stammered.

It wasn't until a few months later I would know the significance of that visit.

MY PARENTS

Before they were married, my mother lived a simple life. She had two sisters and three brothers. When her mother developed cancer, Mum, being the second eldest, took on the role of mother in the family, which continued after my grandmother's death.

She met my father one Sunday afternoon while he was stationed in Folkestone where she lived. She was taking her brothers and sisters for a walk. She amused us telling how she sent her siblings home when she found Dad following her. They began courting, and when it was time for my father to leave, he asked Mum to write first. He took a letter with his address on from his pocket. He tore the address off and gave it to my mother, asking her to write first. The thing he didn't notice was that he had torn between the two numbers of the address. When he didn't hear from my mother for a while, he began to give up hope that he would. However, my grandmother called into the local corner shop and was asked if the letter that had been sitting unclaimed for some time was for her son. It was Mum's letter.

Had the letter been returned I wouldn't be writing this.

INTERLUDE IN FRANCE

Soon after they were married, Mum and Dad moved to France. Dad got a job working on the war graves. Dad was a keen gardener. Bill, my brother, was born in France. It was when war was announced that they decided to return to England so as not to be in a strange country during a war. They told many amusing stories of their time in France, especially where the language was concerned. Neither of them spoke French when they went out.

Again, had they settled there, this book might be written in French.

Difficult Backgrounds

Both my parents had known financial lack in their childhood. Added to this, my father had a Catholic upbringing and was sent to a Convent school. His experience was very grim, and he told many stories of great cruelty, some were hard to believe. He was quite embittered where God was concerned because of this. He related unashamed that he had run away and joined the army after being expelled from the Convent. Apparently Dad had seen a nun throw a girl down a flight of stairs. Then, I'm afraid, he and a friend threw the nun down the stairs and were expelled.

Dad found it difficult to show emotion or express his feelings. He could appear hard at times and was quite strict as a parent.

Bill, my brother, spent a brief time doing his national military service, but he was invalided out of the army when he suffered a breakdown. He went on later to receive an award for long-term service as a postman and had three children and four grandchildren.

Extended Family

Dad loved animals. He kept various species while he was in the army. He introduced some into our home. On one occasion he walked in with a mongoose!

Mum and I waited while Dad coaxed this creature out of its cage. He told us how entertaining they could be. The mongoose ran around the room a few times and then disappeared up the chimney. We were at a loss to know what to do, so we put a saucer of milk to tempt it down. Eventually it came down covered in soot, bringing some with it, and ran round the room depositing soot everywhere!

The animal did settle down and would venture out of its cage but showed signs of stress. Dad got rid of it and introduced a large chow dog in its place! Mum and I tried to object to this, but it pined and won our hearts. Dad had always kept caged birds and tanks of fish, even when we lived in the flat. Mum must have had a lot of grace.

Mum and Dad were proud grandparents. Mum was a productive knitter and made clothes for both Bill's children and my Matthew. Like many grandmothers, she found comfort in these children after her own had left the nest.

APART IN EXETER

I found the ten years I was away while in Exeter difficult, knowing the family wasn't so strong in some areas. I would communicate as best I could but knew there was little I could do in some of these areas.

Mum and Dad visited Exeter at times, and I would travel to them. They loved coming down to Devon and got on so well with both Bob and Norah, who always made them very welcome. I enjoyed their visits. They accepted my being there and seemed comforted to see me happy and secure.

A few months after Dave's visit to fix the roof, Dad wrote me a letter, which caused me to think he was finding retirement a bit difficult. I stepped up my phone calls. Mum, too, told me on the phone that she was concerned. It was difficult for me to assess the situation from a few hundred miles away. I did consider visiting, but felt all the while they were coping I would sit tight and would be prepared to go if I thought there was something I could do. I phoned more frequently and found Dad began to open up to me. He shared his feelings and fears. He also shared something that was haunting him.

I asked prayer from those Fellowships I felt confident I could expect support from. I also phoned Dave. He said he would stand by and if I needed him to visit Dad he would go. I knew Dad needed to make peace with God. He certainly needed God. I had never preached to him. The Lord had shown me not to.

I prayed, "Lord, do something that Dad will know without a shadow of doubt it is You."

As we talked on the phone, I said, "Dad, I'm asking you to do something I've never asked you to do before. Will you pray?"

"I've never done that in my life," he confessed.

"Well do it now, Dad. God has waited a long time to hear from you."

How I wish I had prayed with him on the phone myself, but I didn't. I phoned again on Thursday. We talked. Then I asked him, "Dad did you do what I asked?"

"Yes," he said.

"Well, do it again."

He began to cry. "Dad, you need help," I said.

"I thought of the man who came at New Year to help me with the snow," he replied.

"Do you mean Dave?"

"Yes, would he come?" he asked.

"Yes Dad, Dave will come. I'm not going to send anyone I don't trust because I love you." I had never said those words to him in my life.

"And I love you," he replied. "Now I must go."

Those were the last words Dad and I ever spoke to each other.

True to his word, Dave went to see Dad after I phoned him and took another brother with him.

"Your dad received me like a long lost friend," Dave told me afterward.

"He hugged me and let me pray with him." Dave had said he would come again.

Neither Dave nor I saw Dad alive again.

"JESUS HOLDS THE KEYS OF DEATH."

The doctor was called the next day by the family but because he could hold a conversation about his garden, the doctor said that he didn't think there was much wrong with him and prescribed antidepressants and sleeping pills. Unfortunately, late Sunday night Dad took the lot. When I phoned Dave to tell him Dad was dead, he was shocked but was a great help and comfort to me.

"Jesus holds the keys of death," he said.

It was the first time in his entire life that Dad had softened and turned toward God. Mum said it was the first time she had ever seen him cry.

I leave my father's final moments and destiny with God. Jesus holds the keys of death and hell. He knows.

ALONE

During this time I was undergoing an extremely painful experience and situation in the Fellowship in Exeter. I was so grateful for Dave's love at a time when I needed it. On the morning Mum phoned to tell me that Dad had died, I was numb. I was due to baby-sit for John and Heather, a dear couple in the Fellowship who I was particularly close to. I phoned Heather to say I wasn't able to come that evening. I told her what had happened.

A little while later Pat, known for her work with Mr. North's writing, came to the door.

"Is there anything I can do?" she asked.

Not knowing what to say, I replied, "Just sit with me while I pack." I was going to make my way by train to my brother's home in Dulwich, London, where my mother had been taken.

Pat sat in the rocking chair in my bedroom, and I talked when I felt like it or remained lost in my thoughts. I just appreciated her being there. After a short time, the phone rang.

Heather said, "John is on his way home from work. He is driving you to London. Be ready in about an hour, have something to eat here, and go with him."

I was never more relieved.

"I so wanted that for you," Pat said.

She waited with me until John arrived. He took me to London and then drove all the way back to Exeter the same day. I shall never forget his kindness.

THE FUNERAL

As the day of Dad's funeral approached, I was concerned for Mum. It was to be a cremation, and I knew it could be very stark when the coffin suddenly disappeared. I prayed for Mum and asked the Lord to support her in case she found it too emotional.

It was a sunny day when we gathered in the little crematorium. After singing a hymn and listening to a short address, I noticed the minister looked concerned and kept glancing toward the back of the room. He eventually stepped forward and indicated that we should follow him. The coffin was still sitting at the front with curtains on either side of it. We filed past and walked out through a doorway to the left. I remember thinking how dignified it all seemed and unlike any other cremation I had been to before.

RECOGNIZING THE HAND OF GOD, I QUICKLY ASSURED HIM.

Afterward, the family came back to Mum's house where I had prepared a buffet. We had just started eating when the funeral director came to the door. He entered the lounge and made an announcement, "I'd like to apologize that the curtains wouldn't pull closed this afternoon." He said, "It has never happened before."

Recognizing the hand of God, I quickly assured him, "We preferred it that way."

My brother added just as quickly, "Yes, we preferred it that way."

I knew that my prayer had been answered!

Another answered prayer was that the thing haunting Dad had left after Dave prayed for him. Over tea after the funeral, an uncle, Dad's brother, asked me who had visited Dad. I told him and said, "I think he was a help to Dad,"

"So I hear," was my uncle's confirmation.

Mum stayed with my brother and sister-in-law until after Dad's funeral then eventually went back to her home. She and her brother decided to live together as he was also on his own. Unfortunately it didn't work out. My uncle left. Mum wasn't able to cope with life without Dad, so my brother Bill arranged for her to go into care home. I knew if I had tried to care alone for Mum it would have been disastrous for us both. By this time my life had taken a different course and I was living in Scotland. I did visit from there on one occasion before the home was given up. After that, I didn't see my mother alive again. Nor was I fit to attend her funeral when she died in 1988.

FREE TO LOVE

After my conversion and release into the life of God, I found my heart was free to love in a new way. Emotional needs and a sense of guilt where my parents had been concerned were gone. I no longer blamed them or felt I owed them more than to love them. I told Mum on one of the last occasions I saw her that God had brought me to peace where Matthew and my past were concerned.

"I know that," she confirmed, "and Dad knew it too before he died."

I felt relieved that there was such a measure of understanding between us.

I wrote once while I was in Exeter, asking them to forgive the grief my life had brought them. God put it in my heart to tell them this, along with what He had done for me.

Dad wrote back saying, "I'm glad you've found what you are looking for."

I knew that accepting the situation brought them peace, and I'm grateful they found the grace to understand. I'm grateful too for all they did for me and taught me.

Chapter Fourteen

Faith, not Resolutions

...Whither shall I flee from Thy presence?
If I take the wings of the morning
And dwell in the uttermost parts of the sea,
...Thy right hand shall guide me.[1]

THE ROAD NORTH

In the autumn of 1979, Norah was to drive Dot all the way to Scotland to make arrangements for her forthcoming move there. Mr. and Mrs. North had already left Exeter and moved to Auchenheath. They were to be followed by Dot, who was still involved full time with the recording of Mr. North's ministry. Plans were under way for her to move up there; quite an undertaking with all her equipment.

One morning the phone rang. It was Norah, "While I was praying this morning, the Lord put it into my heart to invite you to come with us to Scotland for a few days' holiday. Phone me back in ten minutes to let me know whether you'll come!"

At that time I was taking in sewing and had commitments to various folk in the Fellowship, although I was no longer attending the meetings. I was usually kept busy, but when I took stock, there was nothing to prevent me from going. I phoned and accepted. It must have been quite a challenge for Norah to drive all that way herself, in those days, without the standard of roads there are now.

A few days later saw us on the long journey north.

Auchenheath House stood within its own beautiful grounds. The house was approached by a drive, at the entrance of which was a lodge where Mr. and Mrs. North now lived. While I was there, Jack and Eileen Kelly, whose home it was, asked to speak with me in the study. They put it to me that they'd like me to consider moving there to join them in their work. I don't know what they must have thought—I didn't answer them. I just stared, at a complete loss, into the lovely log fire in Jack's study. How could I make such a decision alone? Leave Exeter, and all I knew and loved, for Scotland? Had it not been for the kindness they showed, I would have felt I was to be exiled.

In his wisdom, Jack said, "You don't have to make a decision now. Go home and think about it and phone and let me know."

Back home, Scotland seemed a long way away and the decision was shelved.

Then, alone on New Year's Eve, sitting at the kitchen table, I was praying and thinking about the coming New Year. I considered my position and options, or lack of them, where the future was concerned. Miss Mortimer was now in a retirement home and the family was not putting me under pressure while I made up my mind about the future. I hadn't spoken to Jack Kelly since his invitation to Scotland. This was not because of procrastination, but uncertainty.

I prayed, "Lord, I can't go into the New Year without making some decision." I rose and picked up the phone. I hadn't taken into consideration the significance of it being New Year's Eve in Scotland.

"Jack, I'd like to avail myself of your kind offer of joining you up there," I started. "Don't make a decision," he wisely advised. "Come for three or four weeks first to see how you feel."

With this in view, I prepared. I hadn't given a thought as to how I'd get to Scotland. Mel, a lovable, impetuous Irish brother whose love I was sure of, along with his wife's, informed me, "I'm taking you to Scotland, and I'm borrowing Tony's car; it's better than mine."

Packing just what I thought I'd need, I left everything in Exeter on hold and started out with Mel. The prospect of staying in a Fellowship house seemed daunting for me after my experience in Exeter. I didn't feel I could commit myself again or trust anyone and needed space and time to myself. I knew this would be difficult in a home where the folk lived communally. I decided to put my fears for myself away and keep my heart open to whatever the Lord would have for me.

On my arrival at Auchenheath House, Eileen, Jack's wife, told me that Steve and Anne, whom I had met whilst there previously, had asked if I could stay with them in Lanark, a town about seven miles away. This would mean travelling each day by bus to help in the house, mainly, I understood, in the kitchen. This I did.

"THE WAY TO KEEP THE WORLD OUT OF YOUR LIFE IS BY
BEING FULLY INVOLVED IN THE LORD'S WORK."

It was good to have Mr. and Mrs. North in the Fellowship. Mr North would speak in most meetings when he was there. On one such occasion. He was speaking and something he said went straight into my heart.

He said, "The way to keep the world out of your life is by being fully involved in the Lord's work."

I knew God was speaking to me. It seemed the key to my situation. God was giving me an opportunity of being involved in what He was doing in Auchenheath.

I decided to stay. I told Jack, who seemed pleased.

It was on this word from the Lord that I moved from Exeter to Scotland.

One of the sisters there, Joy, was going to visit her father near Exeter and invited me to join her for the journey and bring my belongings back. We travelled together; and while Joy visited her father, I packed, sorted out the things I needed, and said goodbye to my friends in Exeter. It was hard to leave many, but as God had spoken, I felt more confident of what I was doing.

As I left Tony and Sheila I felt brokenhearted. It wasn't the way I wanted to leave them. I didn't know if or when I'd see them again. Tony and Sheila were special to me. They had bought number 21 from Pete and Joy Palmer, and they and their family had come to Christ soon after I had invited their children to a Sunday school Christmas party. I helped Gordon and his wife, Chris, who ran the Sunday school.

"Is it all right to invite the children next door to the party?" I asked Gordon.

"I'll think about it and let you know," he promised.

True to his word, a few days later he gave me the go-ahead. He didn't seem to question the ethics of the children not being members of the church. Because of Gordon's big, nonlegalistic heart, now after 30 years the whole family are not only Christians but are married to Christians with families who are part of the church.

GOODBYE TO EXETER

Joy arrived the night before we left so I could pack my things into her car. She stayed overnight and the next day we set off for Scotland.

I was to continue living with Steve and Anne in Lanark. They had twin boys of three months and a toddler of about two years. Steve was a teacher in the local grammar school. It was into this family home that the Lord placed me. This meant I didn't need to live in Auchenheath House at first. Originally I had come to help in the house, going each day by bus. This doesn't seem much of a challenge, but the bus stop was at least a 30-minute walk into town, in all weather, and the bus only ran once every two hours. On the occasions I missed it, I would have to walk from phone box to phone box to find one working, feeling uncomfortable, knowing someone would have to drive to collect me.

I had never lived in the country before and the feeling of isolation unsettled me. As I looked around at the unfamiliar scenery on the bus, being surrounded by fields instead of houses, made me feel strangely insecure. No one knew, but I often wept as I walked to the bus stop.

I had become used to earning my spending money latterly in Exeter and was aware I would have to start looking to the Lord again where money was concerned. The bus fare was just 50 pence per day in those days. Not exactly a fortune but when you don't have even that much, it means trusting God on a day-to-day basis. I could fill pages with testimonies of how God provided for me, often at the last moment. At the end of a day's work in Auchenheath House, I had to wait to see who could take me back to Lanark. There were no buses in the evenings.

SCOTLAND

Auchenheath House, an enormous building, was beautiful, set in its own grounds with a river running through them, in which baptisms were held. The house was rambling inside and rooms ran in all directions like a rabbit warren,[2] as we would joke. Meetings were held in a large room at the front. On Sundays, everyone stayed for lunch, as they did in Exeter. In this house, there was a huge dining room where as many as fifty could be seated at the five sets of tables. Instead of a lounge there was a large library. Book shelves lined one side from floor to ceiling. The kitchen was in two parts with an Aga (stove) in one. In the winter big log fires blazed in the main rooms. Later these were replaced by closed-in fires; more efficient, even if not so attractive.

After a little while someone asked me, "What is it like living with a younger couple with three small children?"

I said in all honesty, "If I ever lost sight of the fact it must be as difficult for them to have me live with them, as it is for me at times, it wouldn't work." We don't need three small children for this to be the case.

It must have been about 18 months that Steve and Anne shared their home with me. Toward the end of this time, they had begun to prepare for what they felt the Lord was calling them to, which was to go abroad as missionaries. I remember seeing a principle of Christian living. Anne planted vegetables and plants in the garden. At first I thought it strange, as they were contemplating going abroad. When I considered this, though, I saw how we must live to the full in our circumstances here, but be planning and getting ready to go when the trumpet sounds!

***

WE MUST LIVE TO THE FULL IN OUR CIRCUMSTANCES HERE, BUT BE PLANNING AND GETTING READY TO GO WHEN THE TRUMPET SOUNDS!

***

Before their plans were settled as to where they were going, the arrangement we had came to an end, and Steve said it was time for me to move on. For the first six months, I stayed with Norah (not Love) who owned her own home on the other side of the valley from the fellowship house. It was then put to me by the elders that I should move into the house.

Jack and Eileen were giving me the opportunity of a fresh start, but it had come at a time that, for me, seemed too late. I was aware that although the beautiful house and lovely grounds with companionship surrounded me, inside there was an aching void. I had never felt settled in Scotland, with no sense of belonging, despite my Scottish ancestry.

Amy Carmichael's words, "In acceptance lieth peace," were a great blessing to me, and I did try to accept and embrace the situation with all its peculiarities. As a brother has said since, "If we go anywhere with an agenda, we'll be disappointed."

I sought to sow my life in every way I found I was able to within the Fellowship. Mostly I worked in the kitchen with Marian, who had lived with Jack and Eileen for many years. Known as Aunt Marian to many, this sister worked tirelessly with a calm, serene disposition. She kept the wheels well-oiled in the house and had a sure-footed walk with the Lord, which provided a comfortable reassurance to many, myself included. The fact that she didn't ask questions gave me a sense of ease with her.

Weddings were beautiful occasions in Auchenheath. In the summer the lawn was set with tables around the outside while the service was held in the center, under a large beech tree. In the winter or when the weather was uncertain, the whole house provided the backdrop. Furniture was moved into the garage and everywhere decorated with flowers.

Anna, who arranged the flowers, had done them for years. Knowing I had done a little flower arranging in Exeter, she invited me to join her. Although her standard was very high, we worked well together. I enjoyed doing the flowers, as I did on other occasions.

There were several single people living in the house and many visitors came to stay. Auchenheath was in a country village and those who lived in places like Glasgow or Edinburgh would come for the weekend to be there for the meetings.

In the village there was a building project. A disused shop/pub had been bought by the Fellowship and was being renovated to become a coffee shop as an outreach. Teams of men from the church worked daily on this. Hence there was a party of hungry men who came in for lunch each day. There were often as many as twenty-four at mealtimes, which meant there was plenty to do. Cooking was not a problem for me, but there were other pressures upon my life.

It was discovered that I was able to cut men's hair. I could be called upon to do this at a moment's notice. On one occasion as one after another, seeing me with my scissors, asked for theirs to be cut, I ended up doing seven heads of hair! All this could be while I was trying to attend to a meal in the kitchen next door.

WORK CAN OFTEN BE A GREAT WAY OF FEELING USEFUL, IF NOT FULFILLED. IT FILLS A VOID AND IS GOOD AND NECESSARY IN THE LIFE OF A CHRISTIAN.

I enjoyed sewing and dressmaking. Repairing and patching jeans became a continual ministry. The joke about tapestry knees was usually an indication that I had tried to keep a pair of jeans going a bit longer for one of the boys.

Work can often be a great way of feeling useful, if not fulfilled. It fills a void and is good and necessary in the life of a Christian. However, if the main spring of our labors isn't fixed and our strength isn't being drawn from Christ, there will be a lack of grace for the task and little glory for Him.

AUCHENHEATH HOUSE

Eventually I accepted the suggestion to move into Auchenheath House.

The insecurity, the remote geographical location, and the pressure I felt began to overwhelm me. My former joy had never returned and, although everyone was friendly, I was aware of a feeling of aloneness.

Had I not arrived with pain in my heart, I might have survived. Spending all my life in an English city then finding myself in a remote little village in Scotland took some adjusting. I had no idea this region north of our land was so different. Mixing became a strain and making new friends seemed difficult.

The house was very large and everything was expected to be done to a high standard. There were many demands and everything seemed strangely out of reach to me. There wasn't the ability to draw from the Lord for myself or time for myself. My discomfort was on the inside, it usually is. I didn't feel unwell, but jobs began to take longer.

I knew I was losing ground spiritually. I had to think about what I did. Adjusting to other people's methods didn't bother me so much as keeping up and coping. Where I could have multitasked before, chores became major events and required great effort.

For a while, on moving into the house, I slept in a bedroom where the young sisters would sleep when they stayed during the weekends. It was often good to be with them and bedtime was frequently a time of fun and fellowship. The room doubled up on Sundays to be used by nursing mothers or for sleeping babies. This meant periods during the day when the bedroom was out of bounds with no privacy. For a person who could relax anywhere in the midst of a house full of people, it would have been no problem, but for me, I was glad when I could retreat into the room at the end of the day.

Later I was given a small bedroom of my own on the ground floor off the ladies' cloakroom.

Even with this privacy, I still began to feel there was no escape. This was because of my own great sense of feeling alone and at sea, whilst still giving out to others, rather than anyone else putting pressure on me.

Mealtimes became a nightmare in the large dining room with the number of those who needed to be fed. It didn't seem possible to eat with everyone without being expected to help.

Soon I found the only way was to withdraw, I began to excuse myself from meals. When possible, I also excused myself from other events and occasions or avoided them. This gave way to prolonged periods spent in my room, escaping. I little realized this was a cul-de-sac.

THE VISIT

One day as I was arranging flowers in the large dining room, one of the elders walked through the room. At the far end there were two doors on either side of the room. He made a comment which I couldn't understand. Almost immediately the door opened again. The figure walking toward me was one I hadn't seen since I left Exeter. I never expected this meeting.

"How are you?" he asked, making a stiff attempt at an embrace.

"I'm all right," I managed.

We said no more; he left the room. Next I was called to Jack's small, private lounge. Walking in I saw the two other elders, and again, the one responsible for my evacuation up north, who had just greeted me in the dining room.

Jack took a seat. I stood blinded by apprehension. One of the elders sitting on a two-seater settee patted the vacant seat beside him. I shot across and sat down. I had no idea what had brought this visitor so far north. This meeting had been arranged but I had not been informed or prepared.

Looking at the visitor and taking the initiative, I referring to former times as brother and sister in Exeter and said, "I did love you."

I heard someone say, "Well, that's a good start."

The moment was lost. I asked to be left alone with him.

We sat as strangers. He made no attempt at opening the subject of what had happened all those years ago. I managed to tell him how he had affected my parents' visits and that they had no longer wanted to come to Exeter because of him. He apologized. We both seemed at a loss for words. The rest of the conversation must have been about the situation that had happened but I don't remember anything of significance being said to each other, and didn't feel any different when the other elders came back into the room. I gladly said goodbye and left in relief.

THE LETTER

Up until this time, my life in Exeter was largely put out of my mind. I felt there was nothing I could do about it. It became both a happy and an extremely painful memory. No one asked, and I mentioned nothing to anyone of what had happened. I simply endeavored to focus on the moment.

After a few years of working in the house, Jack told me that Dave Vine, a doctor and the leader of a Fellowship on the Wirral, in England, had agreed that I should take a short break and stay in the Fellowship house there for a week or so.

I was taken by a sister who was going in that direction. The house was lovely and the people kind, but I felt quite lost and didn't know what to do with myself. While there I recalled that the person who had caused me to leave Exeter had also lived in this Fellowship and, for some reason, I decided to write and mention this to him. Even though I felt wronged this seemed the right thing to do.

I can't really remember what he wrote back. But not long after I returned, a letter arrived unexpectedly. It was on headed note paper and was signed by the elders of the Exeter Fellowship. It told me that because I had communicated with the brother concerned, the action taken against me those years before, had been rescinded and I was welcome to fellowship there.

Five hundred miles away, alone and quite bereft, this unceremonial letter did little for me. No one else, so far as I knew, would have known about the letter, apart from one to whom a copy was to be sent. So far as they were concerned it was over...

But not for me.

MARRED IN THE POTTER'S HAND

I didn't know who I was anymore.

Attempts at normality and mixing exposed me to questioning and well-meant advice. I found myself running away but didn't know from what. From those less discerning, who had seen me as an able-bodied person before, requests were still made and pressures put upon me. The house in those days was extremely busy, with regular Fellowship members but also visitors. Before long I found it impossible to leave my room, not knowing whom I'd meet. There is a limit to how many ways one can answer the simplest question like, "How are you?" or "How do you feel?"

WHEN YOU ARE IN THIS STATE, YOU'VE NO IDEA HOW YOU REALLY FEEL, OR HOW TO ANSWER SATISFACTORILY.

The truth is, when you are in this state you've no idea how you really feel, or how to answer satisfactorily. Gradually it became impossible for me to leave my room. My room became my sanctuary, bolt-hole, and retreat—but quickly became my prison!

I no longer knew how to just be.

One friend who came as often as she could was Helen. Although she was Scottish, Helen and I had met years before while she was in Exeter. She was a single sister who lived in the village, and I often visited her in her little home. Helen proved to be a very faithful friend, and I was sure of her love and concern.

I was still able to do some things. Living in a large household meant there was a lot of washing and ironing. Alone in my room, I had the energy enough to iron. Marian was happy for me take the iron and ironing board into my room, knowing it helped me to have something to do. I was able to slip through the next room to the laundry, gather up everything that needed to be ironed, and leave it to be collected at the end of the day. I ironed whatever clothes I found.

This is how I spent every day for about a year.

Meals were brought to me by reluctant friends who would have rather I joined them. Everyone was very kind, some friends visited me. To encourage me out of my room, a meal would be left on top of the Aga cooker in the kitchen when everyone else was served. I would collect it and eat in solitude in my room.

I didn't know how I arrived in this state or how to get out of it. Neither did those around me, who were very concerned. The situation for those who were responsible for the home became a problem. It became difficult for Jack to let this continue as others were putting pressure on him to do something. Without my knowing it, he arranged for a psychiatrist to visit the house to see me. My communication had become very poor through spending so much time alone in my withdrawn state. I found it difficult when this doctor came and didn't want to talk to him when he asked me questions. But before I knew much more, I was told I was to be admitted into his ward. He assured me I'd have a room of my own to encourage me, which was true for a few days.

It seemed like the end of the world to me. The feelings of failure and disgrace as a Christian were familiar. I had become a problem, I realized this. I was probably an embarrassment as well. Against my wishes I was assisted to pack what I might need for hospital. I was driven away from Auchenheath House the next day in confusion and dismay, feeling helpless and hopeless.

This was the end of the period of my life in Auchenheath House.

The journey was a one-way voyage for me.

There didn't seem a way back. I belonged nowhere.

It felt like another prison sentence was to begin.

ENDNOTES

1. Psalm 139:7,9-10 KJV.

2. A series of underground tunnels where rabbits live.

Chapter Fifteen

Exile

While place we seek or place we shun
The soul finds happiness in none,
But with my God to guide my way
'Tis equal joy to go or stay.[1]

HARTWOOD HOSPITAL

True to his word a doctor had me admitted into a single room in hospital. This was, of course, in the admittance ward with all the attention and care that went with it. I peered out of the doorway reluctant to leave the security of the room. It was two other women patients who took it upon themselves to win my confidence. They persuaded me to go with them and kindly escorted me to the dining room at meal times. My single room was soon replaced with a small, shared ward. The staff were kind and offered support in various ways. One morning, when I couldn't face getting up, the ward sister, Carol, entered the room and offered to help me, by firmly but gently supporting me in dressing. Even making beds with Carol was meaningful. Upon looking back, the care along with a routine and discipline was beneficial.

After some time, I was informed that I was to be transferred to a women's ward in a separate building. My feeling of security was removed once more as I didn't know what to expect. I little knew the extreme contrast this was to be.

The lounge in ward 21 was enormous. Several couches and a number of armchairs were occupied by many women. At one end of the room was a television for those who wanted to watch it. At the other end of the room was a music center and various styles of music would be played. The atmosphere was one of tension and unrest.

On the floor above, about 30 to 40 of us slept in a dormitory. Two wash hand basins served for these women to wash each morning. The dormitory was locked during the day, and the patients had a small locker for personal things in the corridor. To obtain anything from the bedside locker, a member of the staff had to be asked to unlock the door.

Sometimes arguments broke out among the patients and all this didn't make for a very peaceful environment. Some of the nursing staff were quite young. They would use a form of talking down to us that was very unhelpful. In my state, this all seemed unbearable for me. Feeling totally unable to settle or sit in the lounge area and having nowhere else to sit, I would walk. A long corridor ran from one end of the building to the other. I spent hours walking from one end of the corridor to the other and back again. Some would find this strange and it would annoy others. At times my feet would swell from all the walking.

One day I noticed a set of footprints on the freshly cleaned floor. I found myself thinking of the poem Footprints, but I couldn't remember how it went. That evening a patient came to me and said "I bought this for you today. Have you ever seen it before?"

It was a bookmark with the story of *Footprints* on it!

Footprints

One night I had a dream.
I dreamed I was walking alone the beach with God and across the sky flashed scenes from my life. For each scene I noticed two sets of footprints in the sand, one belonged to me and the other to God.
When the last scene of my life flashed before us I looked back at the footprints in the sand.
I noticed that at times along the path of life there was only one set of footprints. I also noticed that it happened at the very lowest and saddest times of my life. This really bothered me and I questioned God about it.

"God, you said that once I decided to follow You, You would walk with me all the way but I noticed that during the most troublesome time in my life there is only one set of footprints. I don't understand why in times when I needed You most, You would leave me?"
God replied, "My precious, precious child, I love you and I would never, never leave you during your times of trials and suffering. When you see only one set of footprints it was then that I carried you."[2]

THE INVITATION

Mickey, the pastor of the little Fellowship in Lanark and his family, along with Helen came to visit me regularly. I used to phone them from time to time on the pay phone. I told them about this. At one point Mickey told me that a couple in his Fellowship had offered for me to go and stay with them.

"Peter and Liz have a small room in their flat and they have said you could have it," he said.

As kind and generous as the offer was, I didn't see how I could accept. The thought of a normal life with a young family seemed impossible to imagine. I tried to explain this, hoping I didn't sound ungrateful.

While I had been in the admittance ward, I had spoken of my need of money to the sister of the ward, Carol. "You need to see Harry," she said. Harry was a social worker and she sent for him.

So it was that Harry came into my life. He was such a dear, kind man. His easy manner, sense of humor, and compassionate nature made it easy for me to open up and relate to him. In sorting out my finances, he had to trace my National Insurance Number as I hadn't claimed anything for so long and didn't know it myself. He continued to visit me and would respond to a call if I needed him.

After some time, Harry came to see me to explain that a doctor felt that I needed ECT treatment.[3] I didn't agree and refused. Harry became an advocate for me as the doctor tried to persuade me to have this treatment. Although he tried to encourage me, I said no. Then he came to explain that because I was refusing treatment, I was going to be discharged.

I didn't have a home, and the only alternative would have been for me to be sent to one of the long-term wards which were there then.

I don't know if the situation really hit home to me, but Harry asked, "Is there nowhere that you could go to stay?"

I remembered Peter and Liz's offer, about which Harry was most enthusiastic. A phone call to Mickey was made and before long, arrangements were being made for me to move in with them. This couple had two small children already but opened their home to me. Harry would come every week to see how things were going. It must have been extremely difficult for this couple to have someone who was in the state I was in to live with them. I didn't find it so easy either, despite their kindness. I was also aware of the strain I was putting them under. After about three months, Peter suggested that I should move on. Harry had been looking for a place in a hostel for me and by this time had found one. This was a sort of half-way house run by a nun and a Salvation Army captain.

My nomadic life there lasted three months.

It was expected that those who lived there should do the shopping, with support. Also we did the household chores. I found I actually enjoyed this. Most of the other residents weren't that keen , so it seemed worthwhile. I also began to cook again. The hostel, Comely Bank, was in Hamilton and near shops that made little excursions possible. It was a strange sort of existence. There was a degree of independence in certain areas. Of course everyone had problems, which limited relationships. Throughout this period, Harry was almost the only person from outside whom I saw. I enjoyed his visits and he would hear of my progress as well as my complaints!

After three months, I was called into the superintendent's office where the news was broken to me that my mother had been taken hospital with heart failure. I found this very hard . I hadn't seen my mother for several years. I had not been in any emotional state to be of help or support to her after the death of my father. I felt shocked, vulnerable and helpless, with a great sense of guilt. Apart from sending flowers and cards, I didn't know what to do. I phoned the hospital and left messages for Mum.

Within a couple of weeks, Harry arrived at Comely Bank to see me. He took me aside and informed me that my mother had died. I was devastated. The fact that I hadn't seen her for so long made it very hard. Harry insisted that he should take me back into hospital.

He said, "I'm not leaving you here. Pack what you need, and I'll drive you today. You need more support."

I protested, but he explained that I needed more support and care than the hostel could offer at this time. When Harry led me out of the house later with a suitcase in one hand and my hand in the other, it was the last time I saw Comely Bank.

RE-ADMITTANCE

Although a different admittance ward, I was again placed into a single room. I wouldn't eat for a few days. But as I began to recover and respond, I was moved into a side ward with others. My bolt-hole was replaced by a small ward with four or five other patients. When I saw the plight and emptiness of these precious souls, I began to want to reach out to them. One woman would lie on her bed and tremble. I sat with her and tried to comfort her. When this dear woman was transferred to another ward, she was so upset she sent for me.

WHEN I SAW THE PLIGHT AND EMPTINESS IN THE EYES AND LIVES OF THESE PRECIOUS SOULS, I BEGAN TO WANT TO REACH OUT TO THEM.

I've discovered even from a place of need we can still give.

I had a couple of the worship tapes that John, who I'll mention later, had given to me before I was admitted. There was a cassette player in the ward, and I was free to use it. Before long, other patients wanted to join me and would ask me to play them.

There was a male patient who only had one arm. He coped very well and would even manage to get items from the ice cream van that came to the ward each evening. This man was a Jehovah's Witness. Although I had never had a conversation with him, he would at times call out abusive and provocative retorts when I was in his sight. I would do my best to ignore him. He suddenly took it on himself to fast and began to refuse anything to eat or drink. The staff did all they could to persuade and coax him, but he was a man of great strength. He flatly refused. There was nothing anyone could do, and I'm afraid he actually died. I've no idea what principle caused him to take this form of protest, but it must have been a dark spiritual one that cost him his life.

I was in this ward for a limited period of time, but before long I was told I was to be moved to the ward I had formerly been in, ward 21! Dread filled me. But this time there was a difference. The dormitory had been divided into pleasant cubicles separated by curtains. The huge lounge had been divided into two large rooms; one for those wanting to watch television, the other for those who didn't. On my return to the hospital this time, I was given a different doctor, Dr. Hudda. When I saw him, I explained that I wanted to be in the community, as I had been for those brief months in the hostel.

"I'll have you put into the rehab ward," he said.

While still in this ward, I complained that I had difficulty with breathing and would struggle to get my breath if I walked up hill. No one seemed to take any notice for a while and thought I was attention-seeking, I have been told. But after some time, I was sent to the general hospital for an x-ray. It was discovered that I had a large goiter due to my thyroid gland. I had been conscious of a swelling in my neck for many years. I was admitted into the hospital and operated on to remove this growth.

I hadn't realized that another doctor had taken over my case and it was Dr. Carolyn Mitchell who had initiated the investigation. The anaesthetist told me afterward that my wind pipe had been restricted to the size of a drinking straw. It isn't surprising that I soon felt much better. I actually spent one month in the hospital before returning to ward 21.

I was soon transferred to another building, ward 28, where we were given our own bedrooms, which, although locked during the day, gave privacy and peace at night. There was no night staff. The building had two or three kitchens and, in groups, the patients would cook for themselves. The shopping was done each week in expeditions by bus to the nearby town. The cleaning was done each day by the patients. The ward was an active one. There was a lot of group activity and stimulation, and the staff members were friendly and kind.

After a while it was arranged that a few of us would travel by bus to a training center in Craigneuk some distance away. This was held in an industrial estate, and the premises held several computers. A tutor would try to encourage us to learn. I was hopeless on the computer then and found it quite boring, but it was contact with the outside world and got me out of the hospital. Outings were arranged by staff from time to time. I very rarely saw anyone from outside the hospital, apart from John, whom I briefly mentioned earlier. He would call in when passing and occasionally took me for a drive.

The years did drag and there didn't appear to be a future. So I tried to make the best of the present.

Helen, my friend who had been a missionary, was extremely faithful to me and would phone often. She phoned on one occasion to invite me for the weekend.

"It will give you a break from hospital," she said.

Helen lived in the village of Auchenheath. She didn't drive so the staff suggested that I ask Harry to take me. He seemed delighted and drove me on his way home after work on Friday afternoon. It was arranged that he would pick me up on his way to work Monday morning.

It was nice to be in Helen's little home, and she appeared to enjoy having company. While I was sitting in her lounge, Helen having gone into the kitchen to make some tea, God spoke to me. "If Helen can live on her own, you can live on your own."

"IF HELEN CAN LIVE ON HER OWN,
YOU CAN LIVE ON YOUR OWN," GOD SAID.

I was surprised by the faith which rose in my heart. I don't think I mentioned this to Helen; but on Monday when I returned to the hospital, I walked into the nearest village, Shotts, where there was a council office. I asked to put my name down on the council list. I was so determined to obey God's voice. They kindly explained that I would need to apply to the area where I'd like to live and gave me the necessary forms.

With the assistance of the ward staff, I completed the forms, putting Lanark as my first choice. Lanark is a small market town. It was on both a train and bus route and there were shops. But the main reason I chose to live there was because the Fellowship was there.

The prospect of living alone terrified me, but God had spoken.

Everyone at the hospital was so enthusiastic, especially Harry, who wrote to the council along with the doctor I was then under.

I didn't know that I was actually registered homeless until then!

The waiting period then began.

MEETING AGAIN

Mr. and Mrs. North were living back in England. A conference was planned, and Mr. North was coming to speak, staying in the house. Dot, who still did the recording, phoned me in the hospital and kindly offered to drive out for me to enable me to hear him. I gratefully accepted. I spent the afternoon at Auchenheath House and went to the meeting in the evening. Afterward John came over to speak to me but I was feeling overwhelmed by being with everyone again and I didn't respond very graciously.

Back in hospital I regretted not speaking more with John and wrote to him. Within a week he appeared at the hospital. He said he hadn't known my address until I had written. He began to visit me regularly and would take me for a run in his car. I looked forward to these visits. Looking back, I couldn't have appeared a very attractive companion, but John always seemed pleased to see me and made me feel he cared. He took an interest in me as a person and always saw the positive and possible.

I WAS FEELING OVERWHELMED BY BEING WITH EVERYONE
AGAIN AND I DIDN'T RESPOND VERY GRACIOUSLY.

Toward the end of my time, the ward I was in was relocated to a large town, Motherwell. An old maternity hospital had been refurbished to house the rehab unit. It was thought that being near amenities was more beneficial for the patients who could integrate with the community easier, whereas the other hospital was in the middle of nowhere. Again, we had our own rooms and everything was fresh and bright.

After enquiring several times, I received notification that the council had allocated a flat in Lanark for me. Although the key wasn't available, Harry drove me out to see it from the outside.

When we moved into the rehab unit, the first thing I noticed was the Elim Pentecostal Church opposite. This delighted me as I thought that I could attend a church for the first time after several years. The first Sunday morning I went to the meeting, I enjoyed it. The church was full, and the pastor preached. I can't recall what he spoke about, but he gave an invitation to respond at the end. Asking everyone to close their eyes, he said, "If you believe God has spoken to you, look at me." Thinking that no one would see me, I looked up.

"IF YOU BELIEVE GOD HAS SPOKEN TO YOU, LOOK AT ME." I LOOKED UP.

As everyone was leaving, after the service, Pastor Potts shook their hands. I went toward him and he said gently, "You stand over there!"

I stood to one side and when everyone had left, the pastor took me, together with a lady from his church, into his vestry. He talked to me and asked me questions.

From the answers I gave, he said, "I don't understand. You are already a Christian."

I looked into Pastor Potts' face and sincerely said, "I need God to do something for me!"

"I'm going to pray for you," he replied earnestly. He not only prayed for me but took out a little bottle of oil and anointed me.

For the next few months I attended this church. The pastor and a few of the ladies in the church visited me in the rehab unit. I found a welcome and great kindness among them all. I enjoyed the meetings and went to the prayer meetings midweek as well.

Gradually I became aware of something happening to me. Being exposed to the Holy Spirit must have begun to take affect. I found within me a stirring and an awakening. Suddenly I could see a future and, on considering the past, I found the ability to say, "I can forgive."

"I CAN FORGIVE!"

It was like stepping out of a prison. I was able to forgive the person who, to me, had robbed me of the life I loved and had caused me to have to leave Exeter ten years before. I hadn't realized how this had blocked, dogged, and affected me all those years.

THE TIMING OF THE LORD WAS WONDERFUL. WHILE PREPARING
FOR A FUTURE, HE HAD RECONCILED ME TO THE PAST.
I FELT I HAD A CLEAN SLATE.

The timing of the Lord was wonderful. While preparing for a future, He had reconciled me to the past. I felt I had a clean slate. With the prospect of setting up home in Lanark imminent, there was suddenly a future. The present was a time of forgetting and looking forward all at once.

I began to live again and have never looked back.

ENDNOTES

1. Madame Guyon, hymn, O thou, by Long Experience Tried.

2. Margaret Fishback; Footprints in the Sand.

3. Electroconvulsive therapy; electroshock therapy.

Chapter Sixteen

A New Beginning

Behold, I make all things new (Revelation 21:5).

LANARK

The time had come for me to think about setting up my new home in Lanark. I had been in hospital for over two years. Not having a family or home meant that I had no alternative.

Sometimes when a new situation is on the horizon, it's best not to anticipate too much. We can't know how we'll feel or what we'll face. To be prepared is one thing, but it's best to be open to God. At times, I confess, I would try to picture myself in the flat and play out scenes in my mind.

The council had difficulty over the tenancy of the flat they were offering me, which actually suited me fine as it gave me longer to prepare and be prepared within myself. I knew it was for an appointed time, but the present was enough to think about.

Finally I got the go-ahead to get the key to see inside. Harry, my social worker, had already driven me there on a previous occasion to view it from outside. I hadn't a clue what hazards to look for. I asked Harry and Mickey, my pastor, to view the inside with me. They arranged to come together. The flat was on the top floor in a block building three stories high and lay back from the road, surrounded by grass, with a car park at the front. A security lock fastened the outside door. Compact and pleasant with a small veranda, the flat wasn't overlooked at all. It comprised one bedroom, a lounge, bathroom, and kitchen. It was as well I had two observant men to help me, as we found the kitchen didn't appear to have an obvious space for a fridge, the immersion heater wasn't working for hot water, and neither was the intercom.

I accepted and signed the missive.

Once the decision was made and an entry date fixed, Mickey engaged some help from the men in his little church and had my flat decorated throughout for me, for which I was extremely grateful. Even Harry gave up one of his days off to do a stint at wallpapering as well. The next few weeks saw me catching buses from Motherwell to Lanark to wait for various council tradesmen. The phone needed to be connected, the washing machine plumbed in, and carpets, chosen with Harry's help, had to be laid. If nothing else I got used to the view from the windows while I spent hours waiting for them and furniture to be delivered. A chair would have been welcome but at least a kettle provided coffee, which I drank while waiting.

Davie, the charge nurse of the rehab unit, had connected the cooker and done last minute jobs to help me. After all the finishing touches were made and I was ready to move in, I was taken across by Davie with my entire possessions, which filled just a few black plastic bags. Soon he drove me across for the last time. I asked to be deposited at the local supermarket to buy my first few groceries.

This was it.

I had never lived alone before.

There was a mixture of excitement and apprehension.

Alone in the flat for the first time, I walked around and surveyed my small collection of black bags.

"What will I do with myself when I move in?" I had said to John.

"Close the door, put your bottom on a chair, and put the television on."

Putting the kettle on first, I did exactly that. The feeling of freedom, of being my own boss, and knowing that sorting out my things would give me something to occupy myself was quite fulfilling. In later years of business and the accumulation of possessions, I look back on that simple beginning.

I KNEW OUT THERE, AS WELL AS INSIDE, GOD HAD A LIFE FOR ME.

Three floors up, alone in a small flat for the first time, I could have felt imprisoned, but my heart and spirit were free. I knew out there, as well as inside, God had a life for me. It was mine to discover. Many things were a challenge only because they hadn't been part of my life for so long. While living in the Fellowships in Exeter and Auchenheath, shopping hadn't been part of my life. Supermarkets really came more into being during those years. While in hospital we did go shopping, but as a group. We would buy all we needed for the entire week in one expedition.

The first Saturday in my new home I took a very large shopping bag and went from shop to shop, buying what I thought I needed for the week. I suppose I stuck with what I had become familiar. The vegetables came from the greengrocers, the meat from the butchers, and groceries from the only supermarket in Lanark at that time. How I got home with this amount of shopping I can't remember. I wasn't aware then that there was a little bus that would take me right outside my door! It was quite a revelation to me also that I could do almost all my shopping in the supermarket and that going every few days gave me an outing and lighter bags to carry.

Those days are quite a contrast to the restrained shopaholic I am now.

MAKING A LIFE FOR MYSELF

The fact that it was August when I moved in meant the weather gave walking an appeal, although I had never really enjoyed walking alone very much. I also continued to attend the computer course started while in hospital. It was when I broke my arm this came to an end. This I believe was what the Lord intended, forcing me to start my life in Lanark. Before long I decided to take up swimming. I hadn't swum for about thirty years. I bought a swim suit and started attending the local pool. For some time I had to make an effort to go alone. Again, I didn't find it so interesting going on my own, but soon I began to get to know the other regular swimmers, many my own age. I now love swimming, and it has become an important part of my life.

I was certain there was a lot to learn and that I would face things that would need to be overcome. This proved true when, within a few months of moving into the flat, I fell out of the bath one night and broke my arm. God must have put a survival instinct into us for such occasions; as upon reflection, I could have phoned my pastor but, in my state of shock, when I couldn't think what to do and being more used to dialling John's number, it was his I rang. It was nine o'clock at night. John came over and drove me to the Accident and Emergency department of the local hospital. It was confirmed that I had broken my arm and I was to be kept in overnight and a plaster cast was put on. It was a difficult break which had to be reset a couple of weeks later. This time I was kept in for a month. I had an extremely uncomfortable and painful external fixation attached to the outside of my arm. After my discharge, a nurse came each day for a week or so. I was also given Lorna, a young home helper, who became a close friend and who came to Christ in my little home as a result a few years later.

EVEN A BROKEN ARM CAN TURN INTO A BLESSING IN GOD'S HANDS!

Even a broken arm can turn into a blessing in God's hands!

In the early days, John not only dropped in for cups of tea while passing by, he became a frequent visitor on Saturday afternoons. Picking me up, he would take me for a drive and, in return, I would cook an evening meal. Having an appreciative companion gave incentive and cooking more appeal, although cooking for myself never lacked interest.

Before long John asked, "When are you going to start baking again?"

"I haven't any scales or baking tins," I gave as an excuse.

"Well, buy some."

"Who will eat all this baking?"

"I will!" he sacrificially offered.

Soon I was looking in the kitchen department of a shop with John by my side. Keeping to the familiar and favorite recipes at first, I would produce a tin each week with my recent attempts for John to take home. The tin was duly returned empty at the end of the week. This arrangement suited us both. Occasionally others were given my offerings, which I found rewarding.

One friend introduced me to a lunch club, which was run by the Episcopal Church in Lanark. This became a regular event and opened many doors and lasting friendships. I was soon asked to take the little epilogue. This really broke me in where speaking publicly was concerned, giving me confidence. There was soup to make and baking came into its own at the lunch club and was appreciated. Gaining experience in cooking for others again gave me the confidence to invite folks for meals. On these occasions I would invite John as well. He provided company and conversation, at which he was good. This left me free to serve.

THE RETURN OF GIFTING

I recall the first time I attempted to knit again. The daughter of my pastor asked me to help her with some knitting. At first my heart sank. It had been fifteen years since I had knitted. We sat together knitting one row each and I soon realized how much I was enjoying this and remembered how much I had enjoyed knitting in the past. I phoned John in the evening, asking him, "If I bought some wool, would you wear a pullover, if I knitted you one?" His reply was positive.

The owner of the wool shop was so helpful and encouraging as I consulted her. When it was finished and John tried on the pullover, he confessed to being delighted, saying he had thought it would be a Farmer Giles effort!

Muriel, another friend, started a craft group that I attended once a month. On one occasion, someone taught us how to make a skirt in a morning. Again having got a taste, I asked Mickey to get my sewing machine down from his loft where it has been stored. I had to ask the man who had a sewing machine shop in Motherwell to remind me how to use my machine. I had completely forgotten, but before long I was making garments again.

MATTHEW

About three years into my new life, John began to ask about Matthew, my son. It had been a long time. I had neither seen nor heard about him. When my mother died in 1988, I wasn't fit to travel to attend the funeral. Mike, my cousin, went and apparently Matthew was there. Mike got his address, somewhere in Norwich, in case I wanted it.

I never realized how much Mike wanted me to want this address.

When John posed the question as to Matthew's whereabouts for the first time in all those years, I found myself thinking, I could cope with meeting him now. Until then I hadn't wanted him to see me! My parents were no longer alive and, as I explained, "Apart from the address Mike got at Mum's funeral, I've no idea where he is."

"The Salvation Army is good at this sort of thing," John replied.

Having friends in the Salvation Army, I gave them a ring. I was put in touch with a lovely captain. She lived not far away and came to visit me with the necessary documents. Beth was a gentle, quiet-spoken woman who became a good friend. I understand it isn't their practice to visit the person being searched for; it is done by post. But Beth phoned the corps in Norwich, giving the address Mike had given me as a clue. On this occasion, an officer from the corps actually went to visit in person. He found that Matthew had lived there for a short period but had moved with no forwarding address.

The search began.

The excitement and expectancy caused me to wake very early in the morning. I would get up, read, and seek God. I believe God used this period in my life to deepen my relationship with Himself. It only took the Salvation Army about six weeks to trace Matthew. He was living in Leeds. The day came when a letter told me he was happy for me to contact him.

I wrote to him.

Perhaps the reply didn't arrive soon enough, so I wrote to the Salvation Army a second time. Not long after, I received a letter from Matthew. He suggested a time in the near future for me to visit him. In his letter he intimated that he wanted a little time as he found it all a bit daunting. I understood and confess, as much as I wanted to see him, that I needed breathing time too.

Mickey and his wife, Anne, stood by to take me. There was a Fellowship in Leeds with which we were familiar. It was arranged that we would drive to where the pastor, Chris, and his family lived, have lunch with them, and be escorted to the address I had been given.

It was October 1993 when we made our way to Leeds. Anne stayed behind with Chris' wife, Shirley, while Chris led the way to the little cobbled street. A small flight of steps took me to the front door which opened into the little lounge. Seeming relaxed, Matthew smiled and greeted me with a hug. After a short conversation with Matthew, and obtaining his phone number, Mickey left us alone.

So it was my son and I were reunited after twenty-four years!

We spent a few brief hours together on this occasion. Long enough really. But I remember waking the next morning with the feelings I recall having immediately after he was born. Oh, I have a son!

Matthew started visiting once a year after that and I would be taken to see him by John, with about the same frequency. He would sleep on the couch in my little flat when he came. I loved these visits, not realizing how God would develop our relationship.

NORAH

It had been many years since I had seen Norah Love. Soon after I set up home, Norah wrote to ask if I would come to visit her where she was then living, in Worthing. She said later that she hadn't expected that I would accept.

However, when I told John that Norah had invited me to Worthing, I asked him, "How do I get there?" The answer sounded simple as he replied, "You just fly to Gatwick, and I'll put you on the plane!" Thus my visits to Worthing began. These made way for other journeys to see friends in England. No big deal for most, but as there had been a time when I couldn't even travel on a bus alone, to me these trips were great achievements and adventures.

JOHN

My friendship with John flourished in the midst of all this activity and enterprise. I confess at times I wondered where it was leading. I had never actually expected to marry or thought it likely, so when John proposed to me I think my answer must have seemed casual. I said yes almost as a matter of course, then realized what had just happened, as I explain later.

Before we got into the swing of wedding plans, I made a few visits to England to see old friends, as I was aware that my wings would be clipped after we were married. John ran a small business, which meant we wouldn't be able to take holidays very easily. It was on one of these visits that I returned to Exeter. It had been fifteen years. It was good to walk around the familiar places and see so many faces I loved. It was also necessary to see how I felt after all that had happened those years ago. In latter years, Norah returned to Exeter herself, as she got older, to live in the house where her daughter and family lived. There were to be many visits to Exeter in the following years and a healing began to take place within me during this time.

I CAME TO KNOW MYSELF TOO. SOMETIMES WE
DON'T GIVE OURSELVES TIME TO JUST BE OURSELVES.

In all, I was in my little flat for six years before John came to live there as my husband. They were happy years, and I valued the time alone. Happiness after that was of a different kind. I believe it was in these years that I came into a deeper relationship with God. Being the first time I had lived alone, I came to know myself too. Sometimes we don't give ourselves time to just be ourselves.

At the back of the flat there were trees. I loved to sit and look into these. The changing seasons saw all the stages of growth and green give way to the colors of autumn and bare branches in winter.

Solitude can be sweet with God.

Chapter Seventeen

Indian Summer

Didst Thou not make us one
That both might one remain,
Together travel on,
And bear each other's pain,
Till both thine utmost goodness prove
And rise renewed in perfect love?[1]
—Charles Wesley

MY MARRIAGE TO JOHN

During my first year in Auchenheath, John Boustead arrived. Probably feeling as wounded and vulnerable as me, he came with his children. His fine young son, Chris, was about eleven years old, and Jenny, his beautiful daughter, was about a year younger.

John's family had just been split by the break-up of his marriage. His youngest son, Andrew, six years old, and Debbie, less than two years his junior, were separated from him. After living alone with his eldest two children in a very attractive area some distance from the church, John was encouraged to move locally. This gave him fellowship and others the opportunity to support him more in practical ways. It was obvious that John found his situation hard and his role as a single parent foreign. The younger two children lived in the south of England, the other end of the country, which made contact and accessibility very difficult. They did fly up occasionally, under supervision. Then there would be four lively youngsters to entertain and care for.

Andrew, the younger son, was a delightful child. He was attractive in looks and personality. He seemed spiritually sensitive as well and would often ask questions and had no difficulty in understanding explanations. This influence only seemed available during his visits. Debbie made up for her position as the youngest by attempting to keep up with everyone and wanting to make herself heard! She was pretty and tugged on her dad's heart strings.

If asked, John's story about this time in his life would differ from mine, but I'll stick to mine!

John and I didn't often find ourselves alone together, but when we did we found we had a lot in common in some areas, although I rarely spoke about my past. I could tell John hadn't perhaps enjoyed the type of fellowship or church life that I had been blessed with over the years. I recognized he had a heart for God, and would seek to be an encouragement to him. Along with this was a desire to identify with his domestic need, having lived as a single parent myself for a while.

I RECOGNIZED HE HAD A HEART FOR GOD,
AND I TRIED TO BE AN ENCOURAGEMENT TO HIM.

We both admit there was an attraction and affection for each other that we probably wouldn't let show too much.

For John, holding down a full-time job, running a home for three, and being an active member in the church left little time for keeping abreast with the continual chores. Dear Marian, who ran the domestic side of the fellowship house, insisted that this could be somewhere the house could be of help. She prevailed upon John to let her include his washing with everyone's in the house. I soon saw this as a ministry I could perform as part of the duties I found able to do. This included sewing buttons and replacing zippers or repairing jeans! I enjoyed doing this and was known as "Auntie Jean" to John's children.

Apart from this, we weren't involved in each other's lives.

When I started to find life difficult and began to withdraw in the house, John would knock on my door and to visit me. He would bring Christian music tapes to encourage me and lift my spirit. It was his time to reach out to me. When eventually I went into hospital, he told me to keep the tapes—they remained a great source of encouragement and comfort for a long time.

He would bring Christian music tapes
to encourage me and lift my spirit.

After I moved into my flat, John and I spent more time together. He called during the day, if in the area with his work, and on Saturday afternoons he would take me out in his car, staying for a meal when we returned. We both enjoyed this arrangement, which continued for a few years. We not only went on outings together, John also met the friends I made of recent years. He never made me feel anything but valued and seemed to appreciate my company as much as I did his. He always made me feel he believed in me and gave me encouragement to get on with life in many areas.

A WEDDING

John and I had seen each other through many struggles and trials and, as life had shaken us into a more normal lifestyle, we began to enjoy each other's company more. We referred to "our relationship" from time to time, but it was early in 1995 that John, going on one knee, actually proposed to me. Unlike John, I must have been very unromantic as, although I said yes, I don't think I realized what had taken place until afterward. Although John had seen me at my worst, yet he still wanted to marry me. This spoke volumes and meant so much to me.

John was all for slipping away and tying the knot, but I wanted the works as far as finance would allow. We had too many precious friends and family not to include them. It took awhile to adjust to the idea of a wedding and the changes there would be in our lives. I was in my mid-fifties, but saw no need to rush. I felt I needed time! I knew from my previous experience that in marriage one has to give oneself. Whereas I married because I needed love before, this time I wanted to be ready to give myself to my husband. We got engaged at Christmas 1995, planning to marry the next summer.

We visited my son, Matthew, to tell him our news, "I'd like you at the wedding. Even more, I want you to give me away,"

"It's nice to know you are mine to give away," he sweetly said.

We wanted as many people to take part as possible. Dr. Jack Kelly, the leader of Auchenheath Fellowship, married us. Mickey, my pastor, gave the address. John's eldest son, Chris, was his best man, and his youngest daughter was my bridesmaid. Mickey's daughter was also a bridesmaid, and our friends' little girl of two and a half a flower girl. She wore the dress I had made seventeen years earlier for Mickey's own wedding, which had been preserved. I wore a deep pink dress with matching hat.

It was difficult practically for either Fellowship to host the wedding, so we borrowed the Episcopal Church where I had led the lunch club for some time. The building was attractive and a friend suggested we use the church hall for our reception. Anne, Mickey's wife, was an artist, and she beautifully decorated the hall with banners and balloons.

It was almost tradition on these occasions for the ladies to produce their speciality dishes. One friend, who was a chef, oversaw the food and made glazed chicken with edible flowers. The table groaned. We found a photographer from Yellow Pages. She proved reasonable and was excellent. When she saw the buffet, she asked for the caterer's card. She commented, "I have been to the plushest of hotels, and I have never seen a spread like this before." They had done us proud!

Norah was eighty years of age by then but said she wanted to do the flower arrangement for me. We ordered those we needed, and I asked our gardener friend if he would have any sweet peas for the wedding. I wanted sweet peas on the tables. "There will be no sweet peas in time as the summer has been so poor this year," he lamented.

Two days before the wedding I walked past the local florist. There outside was a bucket of sweet peas!

"I'll take the lot," I announced. They offered to deliver later that day.

One friend had baked the wedding cake as our wedding present and another friend, who was skilled in sugar craft, iced it as a gift.

"Can I have sweet peas on the cake?" I asked. The search for little vases began. Then Marian produced three little stainless steel egg cups. These were filled with sweet peas and sat on top of each cake. The effect was charming.

Matthew made the first speech and delighted everyone when he mentioned our reunion, then said, "I've known John almost as long as I've known Mum." This brought a round of applause.

In his speech as best man, Chris, making a comment on his dad's habit of leaving things to the last minute said, "Dad was so slow that Jean chased him for fifteen years!" He had asked me before hand about this. It brought much laughter and was an indication of the relationship between us all.

The week before our wedding, the weather was blustery and the skies cloudy. I prayed much for a fine day. The morning dawned to a clear blue sky and the sun blazed all day. It went like a dream. We didn't go in for a lengthy celebration afterward and left in the early evening. On looking back, I can hardly take any credit for the arrangements; we were just the benefactors of tremendous blessings.

John chose the destination for our honeymoon. He had been born and brought up in Ireland and, as I had never been, he took me there for my first visit. The sun shone the whole week while John took me around to see all the beautiful places.

We returned to the little flat I had set up six years earlier, thinking it would be my solitary home forever. We appreciated each other, knowing we didn't have a lifetime stretching ahead of us, as younger couples do. "I feel like a little boy who has woken up to find it's Christmas!" John sweetly said.

Later, more seriously, he summed it all up beautifully when he said, "Just when I thought all of life's happiness was over, God has given us an Indian Summer!"

ENDNOTE

1. Charles Wesley, hymn, Thou God in Truth and Love.

I'll See Him

I'll see His face, one day I will.
Will my heart beat fast, or will it be still?
I'll know as I am known, what bliss!
What joy, what rapture more than this?
There is no other desire or whim,
Than I should finally, be with Him.
The one who knows my every thought,
And with His life, mine own He bought.

Chapter Eighteen

Return and Transition

"...go and show yourself to the priest..."[1]

METAMORPHOSE

Emerging as a person from what seemed to be mental illness and adjusting from a single state to the life God had brought me into was different in many ways.

Has it ever ended?

Being married had all the advantages of a loving partner, companionship, and transport, which had never been part of life before, and a home to welcome people into. John and I had both known what it was to live alone and had always appreciated those who opened their homes and extended invitations to join them at such times as Christmas. We now welcomed the opportunity of reaching out to others, both single and couples, in the same way. In her book *Honourably Wounded*, Marjory F. Foyle[2] explains how a single person can view a couple or family as a source of having their own needs met and to their advantage, whereas a married couple can view a single person as having no responsibilities and therefore, at times, no needs. Neither is true.

A PLACE TO WORSHIP

When John proposed to me, I didn't think of the ramifications. I must have assumed that we would both go the Fellowship I had been in for six years in Lanark, as we both now lived there. However, John still worshiped in the church in Auchenheath seven miles away, where we had met fifteen years before, so wanted me to return there as his wife.

I felt sad as I said goodbye to the Lanark Fellowship.

Returning to the Fellowship in Auchenheath was a challenge but also an opportunity to "show myself to the priest," as the Lord had shown me. I knew it would have some familiarity but less intimacy for me. Perhaps it was time for me to grow up! I had not been in good form in the latter days when I was there. God had certainly done a lot in me since I had left to be admitted into hospital eight years previously.

Would they recognize that, I wondered?

I felt welcomed and accepted and didn't look for anything other than this. The earlier years that I have described seemed hard to recall or imagine. No reference was made, for which I was grateful. Feeling free and gaining strength brought the desire to be involved in serving the Lord, using skills I had acquired. I endeavored to do things the way they were done in the Fellowship and not my own thing.

John and Bill, his friend in the church, had run a children's club for years in the Leisure Center a couple of miles away from the church in Kirkmuirhill, which is where John had lived for fifteen years prior to us marrying. John expected and almost insisted that I join them in this work. Never having done this before and with the prospect of sacrificing a Saturday morning each week, it didn't exactly excite me. However, I soon got into the stride and found new areas of gifting in telling children's stories. As the person who asked me to help in the Sunday school thirty-five years earlier said, "All you have to do is love the Lord and love the children." This became a ministry that I enjoyed, and the children seemed to respond quite well.

ALL YOU HAVE TO DO IS LOVE THE LORD AND LOVE
THE CHILDREN. THIS BECAME A MINISTRY THAT I ENJOYED.

The work continued for quite a number of years. During this time I was involved in Bill's Sunday school ministry as well. Knowing how God had used my own experience of Sunday school and the fact I didn't have young children of my own to encourage spiritually gave me added incentive and inspiration.

At first I continued to keep my involvement with the Lanark Fellowship, attending their midweek prayer meetings. "I have a foot in both camps," I would explain to people who asked where I now went to church. This didn't take from my commitment where Auchenheath was concerned. I gave myself where I could. Baking for both the house and the coffee shop, which was run as an outreach in the village and arranging flowers at odd times was a joy for me, as was taking a turn making a pot of soup for the lunch on Sundays. Marian, who ran the household side of the Fellowship, seemed to appreciate and accept any help I offered her. I did what I saw to do as unto the Lord.

I DID WHAT I SAW TO DO AS UNTO THE LORD.

After a few years, I gave up my commitment to Lanark and tried to concentrate on our own needs as a church in Auchenheath. There was a desire to see the Lord revive His work in the midst. As his life's work had decreased, Jack Kelly obviously felt it. He may even have felt frustration with advancing years. Despite this, he never appeared to see his end as imminent; and when he died, it was a shock to us all, although he was 82 years of age. He remained sprightly and had a very good memory to the end.

TIME FOR CHANGE

It was uncertain as to where the future for us all would lie. No one knew what the Lord would have us do as a church. Jack Kelly died in October 2003. His house, where the church had met for almost 40 years, had been the family home, but no pressure was put upon the group of us who still met there. The house would have been a tremendous liability for anyone to have taken over. One would not only need to know God's calling but have all the resources, financially, physically, and spiritually, and there was no one in a position to do this. Almost immediately, in a business meeting, we were informed that the coffee shop in the village was under a separate trust. The café had been closed for about four years because there was no one to run it. The existing elder and his family were living in the flat above, and the building had been used for the children's work, apart from that it was free. It seemed clear that this was a provision for the Fellowship.

As the Kelly family went about selling Auchenheath House, the church set about restoring the Nethenvale building, for use. There was space for meetings in the eating area, and facilities like kitchen and ladies' and gents' wash-rooms. After a clean and lick of paint, it was ready. There was an air of expectancy if not excitement. It was seen as a new beginning. The building belonged to no one in particular, so everyone, in theory, was equal. Soon the meetings were being held there and lunches were served on Sundays as normal with the ladies making soup or something similar. The church continues to worship there.

At the same time, John and I were finding the Lord opening up our lives together and as individuals. Through meeting Bright, our African friend, we had met many other African brothers and sisters. Two African churches were planted in Glasgow about twenty-five miles away. We were increasingly being invited and involved and looked to where the forming of these was concerned. John was asked to go on a Trust and I found my input was welcome too.

GOD MOVES US ON

We both felt a greater desire for the Lord in new ways. Perhaps, because of visits we made to larger Fellowships in England where we saw God moving, we found a dissatisfaction growing within us. Our church was smaller, which meant we should all have felt needed, but I was discouraged from being involved in the ways I had hoped. Therefore, there was an unfulfilled need within me. I stifled this, although I did express it to John. I waited for him to come to his own conclusion. He eventually saw this too and felt time was passing and the call of God for us to move on. I learned latterly that I suffered from a legacy of an unfortunate reputation that followed me after I left Exeter. In fact, even John had unnecessary things said to him about me. This could account for the feeling of exclusion I felt at times.

We had many contacts in other churches who wanted us to join them, but we didn't see ourselves making a commitment lightly. Having been secure and comfortable in the group of Fellowships we had known for all these years, we wanted to continue in what our hearts believed. For John, it was a matter of dealing with feelings of loyalty too, as he had been in the Auchenheath Fellowship for twenty-five years. He had not known any other since his days in the Brethren, whereas I had been in other Fellowships over the years. It took a lot of prayer and thought, but by the end of 2005 we were both ready to take the plunge and seek the Lord for our future, spiritually.

WE WERE BOTH READY TO TAKE THE PLUNGE AND SEEK
THE LORD FOR OUR FUTURE, SPIRITUALLY.

We met to inform the elders but said we were in no hurry. We had been in the church as a couple for the past nine years. I had a commitment to the Sunday school until mid-January and one of the elders was to be away until early February. Mid-February seemed the time to consider leaving. We realized for some it might be painful, and we didn't want to hurt anyone. We bought gifts for everyone at Christmas and put on a meal for the church when we left, as a love gesture. We made the meal and waited on the tables ourselves. There were eighteen members altogether. After the meal, and while we still sat at the tables drinking coffee, we had hymn books passed round and asked everyone to choose their favorite hymn and tell us why. One young brother played the guitar, and we sang a few verses from each hymn. Everyone appeared to enjoy this. We felt we had done all we could to leave in as loving a way as possible, and the evening is a lovely memory for us both.

A FRESH START TOGETHER

At this time, it was good visiting other churches as there was no feeling of disloyalty. We also spent time together seeking the Lord. We felt the need to do so as there were other pressures on our marriage that needed the Lord's grace and guidance. John was finding running the business a strain and, both having lived alone for so long, adjustment was needed. After a few months, we saw the sense of going to a local church. In seeking the Lord's direction, we considered an exhortation made by one of our senior brothers to "stay in the vine." I had always called myself a "Fellowship girl" and had been in our type of meetings and teaching for almost forty years. For the twenty-seven years I had been single, I had looked upon the brothers as being in place of a husband where headship and care was concerned.

Partly with this in view, also knowing I had been happy there for the six years before John and I had married, we considered going to the Lanark Fellowship. After talking to the leaders, we decided to join. There were younger families in the Fellowship, and we saw the possibility and opportunity for growth. Perhaps being a more mature couple, we could be seen as having something to contribute. Although the Lanark Fellowship was very different from the Auchenheath Fellowship, there were similarities in some areas and certainly strong relational ties. It had been nine years since I worshiped there, and we had all changed over the years. I suppose I expected the same level of fellowship as I had enjoyed before, but soon saw it was not as I remembered, and we both found it difficult to put down roots.

WE BOTH FOUND OURSELVES SEEKING GOD
FOR HIMSELF, NOT FOR A CHURCH THIS TIME.

Perhaps it was time for me to grow up again. This became a reality when I found myself in the center of a difficult situation that we considered was dealt with harshly. Not wanting conflict, we came to the conclusion that we had joined out of haste and familiarity, so we began to seek the Lord again. We both found ourselves seeking God for Himself, not for a church this time. God honored this, and we discovered closeness as a couple and a new sense of togetherness. For myself, over things that had happened, I found my time spent alone with God became precious. Whereas earlier I might have been looking to other people and meetings for refreshment or the need to share my heart with someone, I now found a place of confiding and to "Jesus alone I repaired," as Edward Caswell[3] puts it in a hymn.

CALVARY

For some years I had been working with people with learning difficulties. Part of my job, on one occasion, was to accompany someone to a meeting held especially for such people. This was called Causeway Prospects and was run by a Calvary Fellowship about five miles away. I was so impressed with their love and acceptance of these people that when I got home I commented to John, "If this is how they treat these people, I'd like to know what their ordinary church meetings are like!"

I never ventured to find out.

However, having decided not to continue where we were, one Sunday morning I asked John to drop me at Calvary Fellowship. I wanted to see for myself. I was made so welcome that I wanted John to experience this and for him to hear the excellent teaching ministry of the pastor. John joined me the following Sunday. He liked it all very much. Partway through the service we glanced at each other recognizing this was where we were meant to be; a feeling of belonging came over us. John also discovered a friend there who came to visit us and encouraged us to join. We continued to attend, and within a few weeks it was welcome news to be told that the church had prayed for more mature people to join. They said they saw us as an answer to prayer. For us, this confirmed God's stamp on us being there; the acceptance was irresistible!

It was good to have a completely fresh start together.

At the time of this writing, we have enjoyed several years in this church. It has been an extremely happy time for us. We still maintain almost all of our previous relationships in Fellowships, visiting them and have many good memories. Also, after some time, one of the brothers who remained in the Lanark Fellowship came to speak with us and as a result we were totally reconciled, realizing where the misunderstanding had come from.

It was a great encouragement to me while visiting Exeter in recent years, when I was informed by one of the leaders that after I had left Exeter, Mr. North had expressed an opinion that what had happened to me there was wrong. Mr. North was already dead by this time, and I hadn't known this. Although late, it was a comfort to me and spoke of God's heart and understanding for me.

I HAVE COME TO SEE THAT IT ISN'T ABOUT A PARTICULAR CHURCH, FELLOWSHIP, OR DOMINATION; IT'S ABOUT CHRIST AND HIS BODY.

I have come to see that it isn't about a particular church, Fellowship, or domination; it's about Christ and His Body. It's about knowing Him and His love and being with those who are of like mind. Our hearts are to be open. We are members of His Body, not a denomination necessarily. Jesus is preparing His Bride in all sorts of churches and groups. It was necessary for me to see this and to discern His Body and fellowship with people whom I normally might not have met or appreciated. John, who has been even more closed than me, has basked in the new friendships and love we've experienced in Calvary Fellowship. We are grateful and know that we have changed as a result.

During the difficulties I have mentioned, I spent some time talking to a senior leading brother. When he prayed for me at the end, he prayed that the Lord would "Lead me in green pastures and beside still waters." I wondered how God would answer that prayer. I soon saw this church as the answer. John and I both felt we were meant to be here. We remained, happily in this church for 5 years before returning to the church in Lanark, where we felt comfortable with the familiar form, and changes which had taken place.

> *We are members of the Church Universal, citizens of the Heavenly City. Heirs of that precious Redemption, which has severed us from things that are seen, and made us part of that blessed throng that no man can number "the general Assembly and Church of the First-born, which are written in heaven." Neither life, nor death, nor rite, nor church-order, can divide those who are for ever one with each other because they are one with Christ. Nothing but sin and obtuseness of soul can exclude us from living fellowship with saints of all communion and sects, denominations and ages*[4]. –F.B. Meyer

ENDNOTES

1. Luke 5:14.
2. Marjory F. Foyle, *Honorably Wounded* (Apex, NC: Monarch Books, 2001).
3. Edward Caswell, hymn, May Jesus Christ Be Praised.
4. F.B. Meyer, *Our Daily Walk*.

Chapter Nineteen

Restoration

I will restore to you the years that the swarming locust has eaten.[1]

Many things can be attributed to my restoration. The times I spent in hospital provided stability, with reliable, conscientious staff and routine. The longer period spent in the rehab unit wasn't unpleasant. We all had our own bedrooms and there were no staff at night. We were encouraged to do all the chores ourselves. Some of these were more enjoyable than others. Being able to cook again brought a sense of normality and fulfilment, and having others to cook for gave it meaning.

John's arrival later on, of course, was special. He would come frequently, and his visits, outings, and interest were invaluable to me.

There was no spiritual input while in hospital, but I did attend the fifteen-minute service early Sunday mornings in the little chapel. On one occasion, the minister, giving a message about the Lord as our Shepherd, said, "He calls us by name," and illustrating this said, "Come on, Jean." As he didn't know my name, this really blessed me, and I felt God was encouraging me.

"HE CALLS US BY NAME."

In the rehab ward there was a lot of stimulation. Adult literacy, quizzes, ice breaker games, and coffee evenings were among some activities that helped pass the time and assisted social skills and communication, which I found helpful. During the year I spent alone in my room in Auchenheath House, I had almost lost the ability to communicate. Some will agree that God has somewhat restored that!

Attending the Elim Church, when the ward relocated to Motherwell, was a crucial step. The love, friendship, and acceptance I found brought the love of God to me afresh.

Finding the ability to forgive was the big turning point.

The delay in setting up home during 1999 was a time of preparation for me. Getting used to the idea, wondering how I could fill my life and adjust to being alone were things that occupied my thoughts.

I now had a future and something to aim at.

I believe that the difficulty the council had with the previous tenant of the flat I had been offered was all in God's plan. Normally a new tenant is expected to take up residence almost immediately. We are so slow at times to recognize God's hand. We get frustrated at things He is deliberately withholding for our good. When I finally set up home, I was pleasantly surprised how quickly I adjusted and felt at home. I had often wondered if it would feel like "home" and not just a flat.

It did feel like home.

MAKING FRIENDS

The little Fellowship that met in Lanark was very good to me. When Christmas came, one family invited me to join them for the day. The husband, Stuart, drove to collect me on Christmas morning and took me home in the evening. I enjoyed the following few Christmases with them also, which I appreciated.

When within a few months of living alone I broke my arm, it was not only Mickey, the pastor, but several others who cared for me in various ways. One brother, Colin, who wasn't employed at the time, did my shopping for me each week. He would join me for a cup of coffee afterward.

Every little kindness was appreciated by me and added to the fact that I never felt alone or lonely.

I knew I had a choice. I could live to myself or try to normalize myself by mixing with other people. John quoted his father saying, "If you want a friend, be a friend." Sound advice! Inviting and entertaining friends was a way of establishing relationships and giving expression of myself as a person. I enjoy entertaining.

WORK

A course in Home Care was held locally, over a number of weeks. I attended and, although at the time I felt much went over my head, I obtained a certificate at the end of it. This qualified me in various areas of care.

I had considered looking for some kind of part-time work but wasn't confident what I could do. A friend, whom I had met on the course, phoned to say she had seen a job advertized that I'd be suited for. This was working with people with learning difficulties. The project was run by the Church of Scotland. The main criterion was the applicant must be a Christian. I applied, was interviewed, and, after training, started work. I did have some experience I looked after the daughter of a friend who had learning difficulties previously for about six years. I cared for Lyn in my home one night a week. I found my new job used the experience but I now had a number of colleagues, underwent training and worked in the group homes of the residents. John often tells me how much I have benefited from having this job. I usually have a lot to talk about when I come off duty!

The reunion with Matthew in 1993 and the development of our relationship was significant. So also was my marriage to John. We both feel we have been recipients of blessings from our marriage. We never experienced any opposition on the grounds that we had both previously been married and this never presented a problem to us. When we first spoke with our respective pastors prior to the wedding, it was Dr. Kelly's advice that we wrote to our previous spouses informing them of our intent. I had to contact mine over the decree nisi[2] before John and I could marry. It was good to know I had his blessing.

Soon into my time alone in the flat I started to work with the WRV,[3] serving teas and coffees in the old local general hospital. Later, a new general hospital was built, and I was on duty when the patients were transported from the old one to the new. The ward I was designated to was the mental ward. We served the confused patients with tea and coffee and I spent time talking to them and making them feel a bit more secure. There seemed such a need for them to be understood by someone who could give them some time. As I recovered, I had a desire to visit and work with these people.

I SPENT TIME TALKING TO THEM AND MAKING
THEM FEEL A BIT MORE SECURE.

My duty in Wishaw General Hospital was to work in the x-ray department escorting patients to the various units for their appointment. If I knew of someone who was in another ward, I would often visit them after I went off duty. This meant I visited people I didn't know, many in the mental ward too. On one occasion I approached the charge nurse, who had nursed me years earlier. He didn't recognize me; I had to remind him who I was and explained how I'd like to support patients who were in his care. He appreciated what I saw I could do, but was concerned I wouldn't be covered by insurance. He suggested I train as an advocate for people with mental health issues to enable me to help in an official capacity.

I did this.

The first client I was given as an advocate was in the hospital I had been in all those years ago. Not being a driver, John took me and dropped me off for my first meeting with the client. As John drove up the long drive to this isolated complex, he asked me how I felt. It was the first time I had been back. "Great!" I said. The memory of my long stay there had no effects on me.

My client had actually been sectioned and wasn't free to leave. The first thing I discovered about my client was that he was a Christian and seemed to appreciate any spiritual input I made into his life. My role found me sitting in on interviews with his consultant and solicitor, acting as a mediator. I enjoyed interpreting what these professional men needed to ask and prompting my new friend with the information he had given me about himself and his past. He is still in hospital but is allowed out a few times a year, and although no longer a client, I always receive an invitation to be taken out for lunch on these occasions.

The other client I was given was a woman living more locally. I soon discovered that she too was a Christian, and I found ways of supporting and encouraging her spiritually as well as addressing issues where she needed help. John and I eventually ended up in the church of which she was a member, so we became the means of transport for her and her husband, when she later married.

Two other younger women also joined this church who lived in Lanark. They were sisters and both had experienced mental illness. Soon a friendship and fondness grew and both John and I were able to support them and welcomed every opportunity to befriend them. Again they seemed to appreciate the spiritual counsel, advice, and experience we offered.

In recent years, John and I have found the Lord bringing people into our lives who need help and support. We work well together in this. We see also that as we give out to others together, it brings us closer as a couple. It is so good to see our home used in this way.

Another activity that was beneficial was going each week to a keep-fit club. I'm sure when Paul said bodily exercise profits a little, he meant just that! I think it did profit me to some degree and I felt the better for it and made new friends. Also, being inactive in hospital for years caused me to put on weight. Joining a slimming club was a very good move and, although it took perseverance, by the time John asked me to marry him, I was almost at my target weight!

EVERY EXPERIENCE I UNDERWENT SEEMED TO OPEN
AND DEEPEN ME AS A PERSON. I AM GRATEFUL FOR THEM
ALL AND RECEIVE THEM FROM THE LORD.

Every experience I underwent seemed to open and deepen me as a person. I am grateful for them all and receive them from the Lord, who gives us all things to enjoy richly![4]

Only a few months prior to Jack Kelly's death I asked to see him. There had been an incident between someone and myself and Jack was involved. Being accused of something, I had taken the blame and apologized. It was a case of a miscarriage of justice. John took me to see Jack, and I shared my heart with him, talking over things that had caused difficulty many years earlier as well. We also spoke about his current situation, responsibilities, and his advanced years. At the end of our time, Jack and I fell on each other's neck. The next day the phone rang. It was Jack, phoning to tell me he loved me. Our relationship was completely transformed from then on. In fact, I care to believe he seemed a little happier in general. When his death was announced later, I was very grateful for this memory. It reminded me of the last conversation I had with my father. The Lord has given similar opportunities where others have been concerned.

FULL CIRCLE

Early in 1998, my son's partner gave birth to Leon, my first grandson. I little knew the joy this little child would bring. The joy would be touched with pain as they lived quite a distance away in Reading, England and his partner didn't always appreciate the attention from a granny who lived so far away. Visits were infrequent. Felix was born almost three years later. Their relationship must have been stormy as it ended within a couple years. I tried not to take sides and kept my heart open to the boys' mother, but she was of a different spirit. Some years later she took the boys to live back to Yorkshire. Matthew joined them, living near by, and has the boys to stay over with him on the weekends and some evenings. He makes a good father and shows great wisdom in dealing with his boys. Being nearer means it is easier for us to see them.

These little boys give me great delight. John enjoys them too. They also gave Matthew and me more of a bonding. We could enjoy them together. Perhaps the Lord gave me two little boys as I had lost my own. I was surprisingly at home with them and found them easy to relate to. At times prayer was a release when I felt concern and pain because of the distance and inaccessibility.

Matthew and I have come full circle since our reunion in 1993.

Another personal achievement I accomplished was qualifying for the ECDL in computer skills in 2006. Also, joining a writing group helped me to write, among other things, this book. In my frustrations on the computer, Matthew proved such a wonderful source of help. He is exceptionally skilled at IT. Opening a link on his computer with my own, he sorted my difficulties out for me from his end. When I needed a new computer, he was visiting with the boys and helped me choose one. The contact with him over all this time has been such a blessing and encouragement for me, and I hope for him. We spend hours on the phone talking about computers.

NOW GOD HAS TURNED EVERYTHING AROUND.

My story really started with Matthew and me parting. Now God has turned everything around, and he is proving a wonderful son to me. I doubt if this would ever have been written were it not for Matthew.

The Scripture says, "The Lord restores the years that the locust has eaten." Many have quoted this to me where my life is concerned. When God restores, He does a complete job. He has restored my heart, my soul, and my mind.

To Him be the glory and praise.

ENDNOTES

1. Joel 2:25.

2. Decree nisi: In divorce cases, a decree nisi is issued by the court to tell the parties that they have to wait a certain period of time before making their divorce final.

3. Womens Royal Voluntary Society. One of the UK's largest volunteer and charitable organizations.

4. See 1 Timothy 6:17.

Chapter Twenty

Finally

It is done! I am the Alpha and the Omega,
the Beginning and the End.
I will give of the fountain of the water of life
freely to him who thirsts.[1]

We don't know what the future holds. The Lord has led us and kept us and there is no reason to doubt He will continue to do so.

During 1995, John's daughter, Debbie, visited us for two weeks. Her young man came on the weekends as well. We entertained them in our one bedroom flat. Great imagination was needed for sleeping arrangements as they weren't married. We managed. Afterward we approached the council for a bigger flat, explaining that we now had a family of five between us and at times they visited. I was asked to complete a medical form. I told them I had no medical condition but was told to give every reason why we needed to move. This I did. I mentioned the four flights of stairs, restriction of space, and single bedroom. As a result, we shot to the top of the housing list and were offered a house within a short distance of the flat. It needed a lot of work done to it. The décor had been sadly neglected, but it had a lot of potential with two bedrooms and all the features we could have asked for. It was in a quiet spot with a little back and front garden and in a cul-de-sac, so had no passing traffic.

GOD PROVED HIS LOVE AND GRACE TO ME WHEN WE NEEDED TO MOVE.

God proved His love and grace to me when we needed to move. It is a policy with the council that, when you accept an offer, they give only three days to vacate one property and move into a new one. This was a concern to me. When we applied for a bigger flat, I approached my doctor and asked if I could have a letter, on the basis of my medical history, so I wouldn't feel under pressure over this.

"No," she said, "you're well now."

I went home and prayed, "Lord, give me more than three days when we have to move."

When I phoned to say we accepted the house I asked, "How long do we have to move?"

"Three days," she answered.

I waited. She then said, "Oh you've coincided with a rent-free period and you've got three weeks!" The Lord had heard me.

We had all the Christmas and New Year holiday to prepare and move in. It has taken us a long time to get the house in the condition we like. I had to learn to decorate again after nearly thirty years! We love the house and know it is God's choice. It has enabled us to have visitors to stay, which we both enjoy.

Over the years, among visiting ministering brothers we spent time with was Fred Tomlinson who has a Fellowship in Abbotsford, Canada. He frequently threw out an invitation to us. It seemed a tantalizing dream to think about; but in 2003 I found I was financially put in a position by the Lord to accept. It wasn't possible for us both to go. Norah was eighty-six years of age by then. She too had been invited several times. I knew before long she would be too old to make the trip and I wanted to offer to take her. I had to be certain before I spoke to her that I was able. Once I had mentioned it to her, the die was cast. She jumped at the suggestion.

We planned to go late spring, being told this was a good time in Canada. We met up in Reading on the morning we were to fly. Norah was in good form and we both were as excited as a couple of school children. I had never been on such a long flight before whereas Norah was a seasoned traveller and took everything in her stride.

On arrival in Canada a wheelchair was produced for Norah. I was told that she would be waiting for me at the baggage reclaim.

Vancouver airport sits in the bay surrounded by mountains on three sides. The airport was nearly all glass. As I walked through the upper part of the arrival area, my breath was taken away by the sight of the snow-capped mountains. Only the Lord knows the elation I experienced. I had made it to the other side of the world. I punched the air, spiritually. God had triumphed and I with Him. The waterfall between the two escalators and the totem poles at the bottom greeting me, added to the occasion.

The snow on the mountains was like "the icing on the cake" for me!

I knew I had made it in so many ways in life these days. Years ago I said that I had lost my marriage, my son, and my health. I wasn't even able to travel alone on a bus! God has rebuilt my life and me as a person. I now have a wonderful husband, my son back in my life, two lovely grandsons, a job that I felt I was called to, and a lovely little home where others can come for refuge and refreshment. Besides all this, the Lord has become more real to me—and the church, my family.

THROUGH THE VEIL

At the time of going to publication, the memories of Norah have been made even more precious as, two days after her 94th birthday, we saw her for the last time.

Norah had been in a residential home for a short time following a stroke. She went into respite care each year at the same time as we attended an annual conference in Devon. We were able not only to see her, but to take her in a wheelchair to meetings in the marquee at the age of 92. She loved it!

This year she went for respite early and I flew down, staying with a friend, and visited her each day. I knew one day it would be the last. Later, instead of the summer conference we went to one at Whitsun. While in Devon we went to see Norah in the home, only to find she had been taken into hospital that morning.

The hospital wasn't very far away. When we arrived it was visiting time and the car parks were full with cars cruising around trying to find a space. On top of this, the parking meters all seemed to be broken. We thought that Norah's family would certainly be with her and weren't sure our visit would be well-timed, so we drove a short distance for a cup of tea. Upon our return there were plenty of parking places. As we entered the hospital, I asked the Lord to undertake where intruding with the family was concerned. Arriving in the small ward, we were shown to where the curtains were drawn around Norah's bed. We were alone with her. It was obvious her life was drawing to a close.

I leaned over her and said, "Norah, it's Jean."

I saw her lips form my name. "Can you hear me?"

Her eye lids flickered as she tried to open them.

I kissed her cheek, stroked her hair and held her limp hand. I told her we were at a conference. I had been told that all the while a person is alive their spirit is sensitive. Also, it is known that the hearing is the last thing to go.

"I love you," I told her. "Thank you for everything. You have taught me so much. We've had such fun, haven't we? Do you remember us going to Canada to see Fred?"

One corner of her mouth lifted slightly as if in an attempt to smile. Her thumb caressed the back of my hand.

The nurse had pointed to a plastic cup with little sponges on sticks with which we could moisten her lips. I took a sponge, dipped it into the water and held it to her lips. She sucked weakly. Putting it back I said, "Norah, you're going to be with Jesus. Ask Him in your heart to take you."

I didn't feel it was appropriate to pray but quoted John 14 to her.

"Let not your heart be troubled...In My Father's house are many mansions...I go to prepare a place for you..."

At this, life came into her face as her spirit responded.

"You talk to her," I said to John.

Norah and John were very fond of each other.

"Hello Norah, it's John," he said, standing over her. Her whole body responded at his voice.

I was about to give her another little drink, when Mike, her son-in law, appeared inside the curtains.

"Hello, how lovely to see you!" he said to us.

"We came down for the conference," we explained.

"Well, it's nice to see you."

We were pleasantly surprised at his response at us being there. John sprang up and, shaking his hand said, "It's good to see you, too."

I leaned across and shook his hand, too. "We are going back on Thursday," I said. "I don't know if..." I couldn't get the words out. Mike shrugged his shoulders in equal uncertainty. "You will let us know..." with this, we left.

I had told our hosts that we might be late for the meal. It was rush hour but the route we took wasn't busy and we found ourselves only fifteen minutes behind the others already eating. We shared with Malcolm and Christine the leaders, who had known Norah longer than me, how we had found her, which was announced in the evening meeting. Prayer and thanks were made for her. Christine prayed a beautiful prayer of thanks and simply asked the Lord to take Norah. In the morning when I phoned the hospital to enquire about Norah I was told to phone her next of kin. I asked John to phone for me.

Mike answered, and I heard John say, "It was good to see you yesterday, Mike."

He gave John the news. Norah went to be with her Lord a few hours after our visit, and Christine's prayer.

Her thanksgiving service, held two weeks later, was special for us as it was our wedding anniversary. We wouldn't have spent it any other way and remembered her arranging the flowers for our wedding at the age of 80! In recent years with restricted contact and visits, I had asked the Lord to let me see her before He took her. He heard. No man could have arranged the events as He did. To use Norah's own words, "It was like closing the book on this chapter of my life."

THE LAST STRAW–SAVED BY GRACE

It was the last day in July this year, the date the conference would start, had we been going. The bedding plants were long overdue for planting. Hastily pushing them into the containers in the back garden, I made to go in for lunch. Then my eye caught tufts of grass cheekily growing out of the container beside the back door. I stopped, not wanting them to escape, and bent to pull one out. It was stubborn, and I overbalanced and landed hard against the outside tap on the wall.

As I FELL, I COMMITTED MYSELF TO GOD.

As I fell, I committed myself to God. I managed to catch myself from going down with my arm against the wall and was able to lever myself upright. I was not only aware I had done damage to myself, I realized I couldn't breathe, in or out. I got into the kitchen and everything seemed a bit surreal.

I thought, If I'm not breathing, I must be going to die!

My mind was crystal clear, and I felt no fear or panic. My next absurd thought was that it was a bit inconvenient at the moment, as unfinished things in my life flashed before me. I had a calm sense of the Lord's assurance that this was not my time.

My spirit rose and I said, "No, I'm not!" and had the presence of mind to "pant." It was as if everything kicked into reality. John appeared from the lounge to go upstairs, so caught sight of me as I gestured to him.

"What have you done?"

"Can't breathe, can't talk," I panted.

Then I signaled for him to slap me on the back, thinking it would bring my breath back. Fortunately he couldn't understand and didn't. In the lounge I couldn't really sit down. Remembering I was due at work at 3 P.M. I whispered for John to phone so I wouldn't let them down. Later John said he had no idea how badly hurt I was. I panted phone 24 (NHS 24). I didn't think to phone 999[2]!

Time seemed to stand still. I felt a lump on my right shoulder and had the detached thought that it was not my problem, feeling confident that someone would sort it out. It was, in fact, the oxygen from my collapsed lung. My neck for the next few days felt like bubble wrap!

After a while I could hear the sirens of the ambulance. I felt relieved, then saw John still had his slippers on. Knowing the paramedics wouldn't waste time, I panted, "Put your shoes on!" My mind was quite clear and calm.

The two paramedics were brilliant. When the oxygen mask was placed on my face I felt the relief immediately. As I was able to walk, I held one man's arm while the other carried the oxygen as we made our way up the garden path.

"She's broken the tap, it's leaking!" commented one man to the other.

"Tell my husband to turn off the water indoors." I joined in.

Lying down in the ambulance was difficult. John was told not to try to follow and we were off. From where I was laying, I followed the route by recognizing the house roof tops. This kept my mind focused.

"Don't take any notice of the siren." The paramedic inside said, as we approached busy Wishaw High Street. I had an enormous sense of gratitude as we drove non-stop, knowing vehicles were making way for us.

"We're nearly there." I was assured as we neared Wishaw General.

Once there I was whisked into a large cubicle and it seemed all hands on deck. My comfort couldn't be considered as I was attended to. X-rays, examinations, and questions were a prelude to a doctor punching a hole in my side to insert a drain. He seemed rather surprised as I thanked him afterward. Another doctor arrived who told me I was "very lucky!" I had broken three ribs and collapsed my lung. John was called and almost immediately the two paramedics reappeared. They had waited to see I was all right. I will never forget the warmth on their faces when they saw me.

I was in hospital for a week. I might have been discharged earlier, but I found getting in and out of bed impossible, then I was instructed on a strategy by an occupational therapist. At home I slept in the spare room, and as I couldn't turn in bed, I woke up very stiff and sore. In the early hours I would go downstairs, wrap myself up in a blanket, and sit the rest of the night in an armchair.

THROUGH IT ALL GOD KEPT ME IN THE PALM OF HIS HAND.

Through it all God kept me in the palm of His hand. When pain seemed unbearable, I knew His strength. When getting out of bed, pain took my breath away. I discovered if I worshiped the Lord as I raised myself, I didn't feel it as much. In pain, singing brought peace and comfort. The assurance I was never alone was real. I've discovered pain to be a discipline. I had to let go of everything, including myself. Accepting help gratefully, especially from John, who not only took on all the chores, but cared for me tirelessly.

We both recognized God was at work in us. Our new roles brought us closeness as we tried to consider each other. I will give no credence to the devil. So much good has come from the accident. The love we received from our church was overwhelming, flowers, cards, chocolates, and meals arrived daily.

John and I know we will never be the same again. As God promises, He works all things for our good…if we love Him. He has also become my song in the night.

Although the life He has given is precious to me, it is contained in this earthen vessel. He is my treasure—and I just made out of clay.

But now, O LORD, You are our Father; we are the clay, and You our Potter; and all we are the work of Your hand (Isaiah 64:8).

ENDNOTES

1. Revelation 21:6.

2. Emergency Service.

Epilogue

Measure thy life by loss and not by gain
Not by the wine drunk, but by the wine poured forth.
For love's strength standeth in love's sacrifice
And he who suffers most has most to give.[1]

Once, a very famous violinist was giving a performance when a string on his violin broke. For any musician this is one of the worst things that could happen. Everyone in the auditorium knew what had happened and wondered what he would do. Playing as he had never played before, the violinist went on and completed his performance.

He received a standing ovation.

Afterward a lady approached him and asked, "How did you manage that?"

"Madam," he replied, "my job is to make music with what remains!"

I'LL MAKE MUSIC FOR HIM WITH WHAT REMAINS.

More than once it has felt as if a string has broken in the heart of this life of mine. I am aware that many events of my life have been unusual. Upon looking back, it is just the way the Lord has taken me. But, while He draws the bow and places His fingers upon the strings, I'll make music for Him with what remains. The more we allow His fingers alone to choose the strings and respond to His gentle pressure, the clearer will be the note and sweeter the rendering.

Jim Elliot[2] said, "Wherever you are, be all there. Live to the hilt every situation you believe to be the will of God."

I have been blessed with so many wonderful friends. Some friendships have been for a lifetime, others for a period. In early days when insecurity would cause concern if someone who meant a lot to me was moving on, I would feel a degree of fear. I quite quickly learned that for every relationship that ends, God brings along another. There has always been someone there when I have needed them.

The verse that God gave me in the early days was Isaiah 43:4:

> *Since you were precious in My sight, you have been honored, and I have loved you; therefore I will give men for you, and people for your life.*

True to all His promises, this one has been fulfilled right until the present time. I have no reason to expect the future to be any different. His promise to carry us even unto old age permits me to be at rest where the future is concerned. In saying this, there have been times when the way ahead has seemed obscure. There have been other times when there has been no earthly comfort or person to understand. It has been at such times the Holy Spirit has been all in all to me.

Faith isn't tested solely on such things as a monetary level. When alone and faced with a situation that no one else has understood or stood with me, my assurance has been in knowing God sees. Jesus captured my heart and has held it through all He has taken me. He knows my heart, my need, and my desire to prove and honor Him.

WHEN ALONE AND FACED WITH A SITUATION THAT
NO ONE ELSE HAS UNDERSTOOD OR STOOD WITH ME,
MY ASSURANCE HAS BEEN IN KNOWING GOD SEES.

It may be apparent how important church and church life has been to me. I was on my own for twenty-seven years before my marriage to John. Church was a crucial part and, apart from Jesus Himself, was what I lived for. This was not just for my own ends but I loved the church, for her own sake and would get distressed if anything seemed other than it should have been or didn't follow scriptural principles. Marriage to John didn't change this. It meant at times the choice of church wasn't mine, but seeking to submit and follow him meant accepting his choice must be God's will.

It seems unlikely there will ever be a time when the church won't be my priority, but through many things I have experienced there has been a necessary weaning from dependence on a particular body of people or specific person. I am grateful that I found myself with no choice but to look to the Lord alone. He met my deepest need and promises that if we seek Him with all our hearts He will be found by us. It was not until later days that I learned the truth of this promise. Seeking Him might have meant crying out during sleepless nights, getting frustrated by those who I thought had let me down and simply knowing there was no one who could help me.

After going through one of these exercises, I discovered needs that I had never truly believed, if I'm honest, could be met by God, were in fact met by Him. Thus confirming that, "All things do work for the good of those who love God."[3] Of course we must see that our hearts are right with Him, not lay the blame on others, or excuse ourselves— "and having done all, to stand."[4]

In the early hours one morning, when distressed, I picked up a book. In the first chapter there was a quotation by Martin Luther, "Here I stand, I can do no other, God help me. Amen." I stood every morning and repeated that to God. Before long, things began to change in my circumstances...and in me.

YET I REALLY HAVE NO REGRETS. GOD HAS USED EVERYTHING TO MAKE ME THE PERSON I AM IN HIM.

Have I any regrets? A few, if I care to think about it. I regret not being able to be there for my mother when she needed me. But could I help that? No. So why whip myself over memories? Any other regrets, less painful, I leave with the One who "knows all my days." Yet I really have no regrets over all that has happened in my life. God has used everything to make me the person I am in Him.

One brother once said, "Live so as to be missed."

The deepest desire of my heart is to live to please Him in the unseen things as well as the seen. One of my favorite verses is, "Whatever your hand finds to do, do it with all your might."[5] This isn't the same as being a perfectionist. Perfectionists are often obsessive and intense. But if we put our all in all we do, and do everything as unto the Lord, He sees. It's our hearts that are important in everything. If what we have done is disdained by man but has been done with a true heart to God, it's easier to stand. There are no negatives in God. All His promises are Yea and Amen. His corrections may smart but will never harm us.

GOD'S LOVE IS WHAT I HAVE COME TO KNOW AND TRUST.

This is the love that I have come to know and trust. What other love sweeps all else before it to reach the object of its affection? Jesus is preparing His Bride. Our Bridegroom wants His Bride all glorious within. Everything we go through, as Paul Billheimer says, is bridal training; it is to purify us.

In Ecclesiastes it says, "He has put eternity in their [our] hearts."[6] We glimpse only dimly at times, but our home is above.

Jesus is coming back soon!

I want to be ready for Him.

Don't you?

ENDNOTES

1. Lilias Trotter, *The Parables of the Cross*; The Dandelion; http://www.unveiling.org/Articles/dandelion.html; accessed January 5, 2011.

2. Jim Elliot was martyred at the age of 28 in Ecuador where he was sharing the gospel.

3. Romans 8:28.

4. Ephesians 6:13.

5. Ecclesiastes 9:10.

6. Ecclesiastes 3:11.

Additional copies of this book and other book titles
from DESTINY IMAGE™ EUROPE
are available at your local bookstore.

We are adding new titles every month!

To view our complete catalog online, visit us at:

www.eurodestinyimage.com

Send a request for a catalog to:

Via della Scafa 29/14
65013 Città Sant'Angelo (Pe) - ITALY
Tel. +39 085 4716623 ♦ +39 085 8670146
Fax: +39 085 9090113
info@eurodestinyimage.com

"Changing the world, one book at a time."

Are you an author?
Do you have a "today" God-given message?

CONTACT US

We will be happy to review your manuscript
for the possibility of publication:

publisher@eurodestinyimage.com
http://www.eurodestinyimage.com/pages/AuthorsAppForm.htm